Christmas!

Christmas!

TRADITIONS,
CELEBRATIONS
AND FOOD
ACROSS EUROPE

STELLA ROSS COLLINS

KYLE CATHIE LIMITED

**The Mother of God of Lovingkindness, a
late 20th-century icon of the Vladimir type.**

First published in Great Britain in 1999 by
Kyle Cathie Limited
20 Vauxhall Bridge Road
London SW1V 2SA

ISBN 1 85626 339 8

A Cataloguing in Publication record for this book is available from the British Library.

Project editor Caroline Taggart
Design by Robert Updegraff
Original photography by Clay Perry
Home economists Jacqueline Clark, Maxine Clark, Jake Hodges, Maggie Perry
Styling by Maggie Perry
Text edited by Alexa Stace
Recipes edited and tested by Anne Sheasby
Additional picture research by Julia Pashley

See also other acknowledgements on page 166–168

Printed in Singapore by Tien-Wah Press

**Half title: This is a silver thaler, showing the Nativity, struck in Hamburg c.1650. In the mid-seventeenth century
the Hamburg mint produced a series of medal-like coins such as this, including several with religious designs.**

BUCKINGHAM PALACE

Mrs. Stella Ross Collins.

Thank you for your kind message of loyal greetings. As Patron of the NSPCC I was most interested to hear of your book. I wish you every success with it, and hope that the charity, with which I have had such a long and personal connection, benefits from your authorship.

ELIZABETH R.

30th October, 1998.

1O DOWNING STREET
LONDON SW1A 2AA

THE PRIME MINISTER

As we approach the millennium, Christmas, the original event which the

millennium commemorates, will take on a special significance for many people.

Christmas traditions in Europe often bring out what is unique and most special to

the individual nations of Europe, while drawing on a heritage common to us all.

Christmas should be a time of joy; but there are still too many people in our

society for whom it is not, including those children who suffer from cruelty or

neglect. The work of the NSPCC is vital in helping these children. I hope that

the money raised through sales of this book may go some way towards giving

them the support they need and giving them new hope in the new millennium.

Tony Blair

May 1999

Contents

christmas Tree

The christmas tree,
Brings lots of glee,
with presents for all the family,
Decorations gleam and shine
oh look this maybe Mine !
all of this from a tree,
bringing happiness to all the famliy,
The presents come with joy,
For every little girl and and boy !
But remember jesus in a stable bare
Think of him coming and why he was there!

by Nadine England
4.N.
age: 8
Bengeo county
primary school

The winning entry in Three Valleys Water's competition.

Introduction

For some considerable time, preparations have been in train across the world for the great millennium celebration. While the change of century brings anxiety over the baffling digital adjustment which is hovering like a giant kestrel over the great trading cities of the world, it also offers many benefits: attractive opportunities for family or community enjoyment, extra prosperity due to new and imaginative avenues for trade, and a much-needed boost for charities. But we should not forget that the millennium marks the 2000th year since the birth of Christ.

While gathering material for this book, I have been overwhelmed by the enthusiasm and courtesy which have greeted my requests. I am grateful to everyone who sent material: even contributions which were not finally included nevertheless proved very helpful. Specific acknowledgements are given at the end of the book, but I would like to take this opportunity to thank my family for great support and encouragement; my personal assistant, Caroline Burmaster, for her friendship and wide-ranging efficiency, and Rosemary Brace for some secretarial help. Otherwise, suffice it to say here that *Christmas!* is the product of unstinting and generous effort on the part of many Embassies, institutions and individuals throughout Europe. The idea of the book even inspired Three Valleys Water plc, who supply water to 870,000 English homes, including my own, to run a competition for local schoolchildren to write about their experience of Christmas. It attracted 140 entries and, in these commercially minded times, it was particularly gratifying to find that the winning poem, by eight-year-old Nadine England, which is reproduced opposite, reflects not only concern for the family but also an awareness of how our Christmas traditions began.

The word 'tradition' means 'opinion, belief or custom which is handed down from ancestors to posterity'. I believe that our Christmas traditions are entrusted to us like the baton in the relay race of life – the safe 'taking over' and the accurate 'handing on' ensures continuity.

The mention of 'continuity' of course brings me back to children, and to the charity with which I have been concerned for over 60 years – the National Society for the Prevention of Cruelty to Children, better known to millions as the NSPCC. It has been helping abused and neglected children for more than a century. Thousands are helped every year and as this book goes to press a major new campaign has just been launched to raise more money and promote even greater awareness of the NSPCC's vital work. As we enter the new millennium, may we do so with greater love and understanding for the needs of our children and of future generations throughout the world.

Stella. Ross Collins.

Christmas Country by Country

There are now well over 40 countries in Europe and contributors to this book range from Norway in the north to Malta and Cyprus in the south; from France in the west to Russia in the east. In some places, Christmas traditions take account of the long months of darkness that surround the festive season; in others, ancient pagan practices continue with a contemporary interpretation. Many features overlap national boundaries – St Nicholas is a favourite saint in both Austria and Holland, for example; the festival of the Three Kings is important in both Andorra and Slovenia; the main celebratory meal is eaten on Christmas Eve in many Catholic countries – but each country also has its individual traditions. The following pages are an attempt to capture the flavour of these diverse neighbours.

Andorra

Father Christmas is quite new in Andorra, a reflection of the fact that the country is now part of an international market-place and promotional clout has swung heavily behind December 25th. In the past, the 'Three Kings' was the important event. 'Royal Pages' visited each parish on January 4th to collect the 'Want' letters – and the promises to be good. The next day, January 5th, the Kings arrived in horse-drawn carriages and decorated floats, and families waited at their front doors for the Kings to deliver the presents.

On Christmas Eve the Midnight Mass is announced by the ringing of church bells fifteen minutes beforehand. Prior to leaving the house, many older folk still observe the custom of making sure the fire is burning and a chair placed nearby. Who knows whether the Mother of God might not choose to drop in and warm herself at the hearth? After Mass, worshippers stand around outside the church, greeting each other while they sip the hot chocolate or mulled wine supplied by the parish.

At New Year, a Catalan custom requires that twelve 'lucky' grapes should be eaten during the chiming of the twelve strokes of midnight. Seedless grapes are probably a sensible choice!

Armenia

Armenia stands in a position of unique significance: it was the first country in the world officially to adopt Christianity. Consequently it is there that one finds the earliest Christian basilicas and the survival of the basic church traditions. Armenia was part of the Soviet Union for 70 years, during which time religious traditions vanished under the pressure of Marxist theory and atheism. However, after seven years of independence and transition, it is indeed cheering news to hear that old customs are gradually returning.

Two important traditions separate the country from the rest of Europe. First, the celebration of Christ's birth takes place on January 6th, which is the date all early Christians used before it was officially changed to December 25th in the year 336 AD. The second difference from other European countries is very unexpected – gifts are *not* exchanged either on Christmas Eve or Christmas Day. It is New Year's Eve when families gather together to greet Gakhand Baba (Father Winter) who brings presents to the children.

Austria

St Nikolaus, as he is generally known, has his day on December 6th, and brings the first real flavour of Christmas. He is first mentioned in Austrian literature in the 15th century and remains very much part of Christmas, probably because he brings presents of fruits and sweets to children who have put their shoes on the windowsill. That is the good news – but sometimes he is accompanied by Krampus, who wears devil's horns and fur and, if he feels so inclined, collects all horrid children in a rucksack and takes them to hell. Luckily, Nikolo can protect them!

Children believe that the tree and presents are brought by the Christ Child. Under the tree there is nearly always a crib. On Christmas Eve presents are exchanged and the father often reads the Christmas Gospel, which is followed by the singing of carols, the most popular being 'Silent Night'.

Belgium

Most Belgian cities and villages have their coloured illuminations around the main streets and commercial centres. Christmas trees are erected and cribs set up in town squares and churches, while carol singers practise their recitals and the search for gifts continues amongst the Christmas markets which are becoming more and more popular.

Midnight Mass on Christmas Eve is the most important Christmas event, from city cathedrals to village churches. These masses are celebrated sometimes very simply, sometimes with great splendour. Midnight Mass is followed by the traditional *Réveillon*, the special Christmas Eve supper. Hares and rabbits were at one time the traditional main course and in some Walloon areas, black and white puddings, but these have slowly been replaced by turkey, at any rate in towns.

Bulgaria

Most Bulgarian Christmas customs reflect the hopes and fears of a farming community. Christmas Eve is known as 'the evening of what is to be'. On December 20th (*Ignazhden*), it was customary for women to refrain from various forms of work, such as sewing, knitting and washing, and as far as possible, cooking, especially in the case of pregnant women and young brides, because there was a belief that the Virgin went into labour on that day. These prohibitions were an act of homage to her and to secure an easy confinement for themselves!

Winter was a time when little could be done in the fields, when women stayed at home to spin and weave, when food and wine were plentiful, when young people prepared for marriage and when the rebirth of the Sun God and the birth of the Son of God were celebrated together in a confusion of pagan and Christian rites and celebrations. Until only a few years ago, New Year celebrations took precedence over Christmas.

The Channel Islands

After the Reformation there were no Christmas celebrations, but since the relaxation of Calvinism in the mid-19th century it has been customary for the islanders to have a whole week of feasting and merry-making. There is an old tradition of ringing the church bells non-stop from midday Christmas Eve to midnight Christmas Day. This custom is continued in some parishes, but there are now gaps so that church services can be held. In St Helier (Jersey) a huge illuminated cross is erected at Easter and Christmas. This is visible as far as the Island of Grouville and out to sea as far as Les Minquiers. The St Helier's signal station puts out 18 flags spelling out 'Season's Greetings'.

Croatia

After the clouds of war, the return of Christmas over these last few years has been the source of much joy in Croatia. Rituals and customs vary from region to region, and from one ethnic group to another. According to the Catholic calendar, December 24th is devoted to Adam and Eve. It is required to be a day of fasting and people still observe the fast, but the long Christmas Eve before going to Mass is also a time of entertainment. People sing, drink wine and tell stories.

Croatians always shoot when celebrating, especially on Christmas Eve and Christmas Day. Young men visit friends or neighbours and from dusk onwards they fire their guns — nowadays revolvers and automatic weapons — into the air to drive away evil spirits.

Cyprus

The Greek Orthodox Church has been the mainstay of religion in Cyprus since the 1st century and continues to play an important role. Old-style values have been maintained and the family unit remains close and helps to keep colourful customs alive.

Larnaca's links with Christianity go back to the very beginning, for its first Bishop was none other than Lazarus, who lived there after Jesus had raised him from the dead. A church built in his name exists on the spot where his remains were said to be found. St Basil replaces St Nicholas as the popular saint at this time of year, and Vasilopitta cakes (see recipe page 150) with coins hidden inside are still made for New Year in his memory.

Czech Republic

Christmas in the Czech Republic is a time to party, to celebrate, to be with the family. Festivities start early, with decorations everywhere. The old Town Square in Prague, *Staromestske Namesti*, is turned into a forest of Christmas trees with animals grazing in a stable of straw. A huge central tree is surrounded by stalls made of foliage, from which gifts are sold.

Christmas Day is celebrated on December 24th and carp is the traditional food. It is said that if you do not eat carp on this day you will see Golden Piglets on the wall. It is lucky to have three fish scales in your wallet. They must be given to you by a friend and this will promote good fortune. December 25th is called the Feast of the Gods and friends join each other to enjoy a turkey. January 1st is lentil day — you must not eat fish or fowl as your luck will fly away, but lentils are said to bring money.

Denmark

Christmas preparations proper begin with greeting cards and letters for abroad. Each year a new design of Christmas seal is issued — a mini work of art. One of the most beautiful was a set of music-making angels, designed by Queen Margarethe. The revenue from these seals (50 million are printed) goes towards convalescence facilities for ailing children.

The first celebration takes place on the first Sunday in Advent, when friends and family gather to drink warm glogg — a kind of mulled wine (see recipe on page 164). An old Danish custom demands that no visitor during Christmas may be allowed to leave without having tasted the Christmas cookies — otherwise there is the risk that the visitor 'will carry the Christmas spirit away'.

England

Christmas as we know it today, complete with turkey, tree, mince pies, cards and crackers, is largely a Victorian invention. Medieval Christmases were much heartier affairs, but with the advent of the Puritans, such jollity was banned, and the celebration of Christmas fell out of favour.

The modern Christmas emerged in 1843 with the publication of *The Christmas Carol* by Charles Dickens, where the themes are family, children and charity, and Bob Cratchit and his family enjoy a turkey dinner which we would certainly recognise today. Fir trees decorated with apples, paper flowers and candles were introduced by German immigrants and made popular by Prince Albert who also introduced decorations made from spun glass and paper ornaments. Cards and crackers were both Victorian English inventions, while plum pudding has been with us since medieval times.

Christmas in the remote Isles of Scilly is rather different from the rest of England. Despite often turbulent weather, it is a quiet affair as expatriates return to their families. Because of the temperate climate, plants indigenous to the Mediterranean countries grow happily and successfully here, providing welcome flowers both for home and abroad. New Year's Day is now the principal celebration, with fancy dress parties and flocks of tourists from the mainland. Many years ago there was a tradition of lifting farm gates and leaving them leaning against the gate-post on New Year's Eve to welcome in the New Year. This is no longer carried out, though there is little chance of cattle escaping as most farmers concentrate on flowers these days.

Estonia

The Christmas holidays have always been celebrated between December 25th and 27th, the most important event being Christmas Eve. It is fascinating to realise that Scandinavia along with Estonia is the only area in present-day Europe where the birthday of Jesus Christ is still marked by the pre-Christian world of Jul Joulund, meaning the winter solstice when the day is the shortest and the night is the longest. Old folklore describes this season as the time 'when the sun was laying in the nest and from that day on the sun started to rise and move slowly to the north again'.

Christmas was banned during the Soviet rule, but was still unofficially celebrated with church services on Christmas Eve. Since regaining independence, Christmas is once again celebrated as a holiday. Each year on December 24th the President declares Christmas Peace and attends a church service – this tradition is 350 years old.

Finland

Finland is the homeland of Father Christmas. Children believe that Father Christmas and Mother Christmas live with dozens of their little helpers, Tonttus, in their mountain home in Lapland. This mountain has three ears which enable Santa to hear messages from people all over the world.

In Lapland there are only a few hours of daylight in winter. Darkness falls in early afternoon. Children can actually travel to Lapland for a meeting with Father Christmas (in his Christmas-card setting). The fact of reaching the Arctic Circle is in itself rather dramatic, and on arrival at Avalo Airport, travellers are welcomed not only by reindeer escorted by Lapps in traditional costume, but by a choir singing much-loved carols about a very different journey.

Christmas celebrations begin with Lucia Day (December 13th) when a young girl wearing white robes and a crown of lighted candles visits hospitals and schools, and continues until New Year. The visit to the sauna is an integral part of the Finnish Christmas.

France

Christmas Eve is the important day. Following Midnight Mass, which is usually held about 9 p.m., families return home and gather together for the grand feast of the season, the *Réveillon* after which presents are exchanged. Nearly every French home at Christmas-time displays a nativity scene, which serves as a focus for the celebration. An extensive tradition has evolved round these little figures which are made by craftsmen in the South of France. Some of the figures are produced in the form of local dignitaries and characters – the skill needed is quite astounding – and the moulds have been passed from generation to generation.

Most French children receive gifts from Père Noël on St Nicholas's Eve, and again at Christmas, though in some areas it is Le petit J'sus who brings gifts. It is more usual for adults to wait until New Year to exchange gifts.

Germany

In Germany, Christmas is celebrated in an elaborate way – customs vary according to the area and its religion. The Protestants tend to have Father Christmas as the bringer of gifts, whereas in the Catholic districts it is the Christ Child who brings the presents. As in many European countries, the high point of the Christmas season is Midnight Mass on Christmas Eve, celebrated by both Catholics and Protestants.

Germany is particularly noted for its Christmas markets, though the idea is now spreading to other European countries. At the festive stands and kiosks every Christmas shopping requirement can be found, from decorations to food, Holy Family figures, wood-carvings, mistletoe boughs, nutcracker figures, in fact the choice is overwhelming.

Gibraltar

Bearing in mind its history and geography, it is not surprising to learn that Christmas in Gibraltar, particularly at the table, is a blend of Spanish and English customs.

The Government Christmas Lottery draw is one of the highlights of the season and everyone joins in in the hope of capturing the prize of £500,000. The Three Kings Cavalcade is organised every year by a charitable committee who distribute toys to children in need. Groups and associations are encouraged to participate with floats for a parade held on January 5th, the eve of the Feast of the Epiphany. The most original float is rewarded with a prize and the Three Kings then visit the two cathedrals before distributing the toys.

Greece

To members of the Greek Orthodox Church, Christmas ranks second to Easter within the roster of important holy days or holidays. Advent is a time of strict fasting, so it is little wonder that the Christmas Feast is looked forward to with great anticipation by adults and children alike. In church on Christmas Day carols are sung at 8 a.m, and for the end of the Christmas fast.

January 1st, the feast of St Vassilis or Basil, is the time for presents. St Basil is the patron saint of the New Year. Decorations consist of bushes with red berries or tree branches hung with baubles, placed in a pot, or simply branches in pots.

Holland

The Christmas holiday in Holland lasts just two days – it is a tranquil, sociable celebration, and although the churches are over-flowing on Christmas Eve, the emphasis on spending family time together is strong. St Nicholas is particularly popular in Holland – the first church built by 17th-century Dutch settlers in America was named after him, and Santa Claus is an English corruption of his name. Children receive their presents on St Nicholas's day (December 6th), but in many homes they may receive a second lot of presents at Christmas itself. Carols and Christmas trees are German customs that have now spread into Holland.

Hungary

Hungary is a country where Christmas is an intimate family holiday, celebrated by Christians and Jews alike. The religious suffering and suppression endured by Hungarians for over 40 years, during the Communist rule, only deepened and enriched the values of old customs and traditions which many people continue to cherish.

Children leave out their shoes on December 5th for St Nicholas, who brings small gifts, but Christmas Eve is the most important part of the celebration, when the Christmas Feast is eaten. The Christmas tree has real candles which are lit and the whole family gathers to see the presents under the tree.

Iceland

In Iceland, the Christmas lights are not turned on until 6 p.m. on Christmas Eve when all are wearing their new or best clothes. The ringing of the bells of the Lutheran Cathedral in Reykjavik, broadcast nationally for a special religious service, is a signal for all to embrace and share greetings for a Merry Christmas. Surprisingly, this special evening with the feast of traditional food is not an occasion for alcohol – there are plenty of soft drinks and coffee. However, on Christmas Day it is socially acceptable to 'lift a glass' as the saying goes in Iceland.

It is not traditional for children to hang up a sock or place a shoe by the window in the hope of receiving gifts from Santa Claus, who is a recent import to Iceland. It is the *Jólasveinarnir* (Yuletime lads) who put little presents in the shoes left upon the windowsills.

Ireland

The traditional Irish Christmas period was the Twelve Days of Christmas, extending from Christmas Eve to January 6th. The latter was referred to as 'Small Christmas' or 'the Women's Christmas', because it was less important than the main feast of December 25th which was boldly known as 'the Men's Christmas'!

'Bringing home the Christmas' from the local town was a great annual occasion, where home-produced goods such as butter, eggs, fowls and farm produce were exchanged for shop foods and drinks, as well as clothes, toys for the children and household gear. Boxing Day is of great social importance with horse-racing in Northern Ireland at the Maze racecourse and at Leopardstown in the Republic when 'the world and his wife' are out and about.

Italy and Sicily

It is generally believed that Christmas becoming the celebration of the birth of Christ originated in Rome towards 350 AD. Rome also was the first city to celebrate Christmas on the chosen date of December 25th. Before families go to the crowded churches for Midnight Mass (and it is quite usual for children and babes in arms to accompany their parents), everyone sets up the crib, both in churches and homes.

The twenty-four hour fast preceding Christmas Eve ends with an elaborate feast. Small presents are drawn from the Urn of Fate but Infant Jesus or Father Christmas delivers presents on the night of December 24th in the traditional way.

Latvia

In Latvia Christmas is called Winter Festival, and although it has a strong religious flavour, some old pre-Christian folk traditions of celebrating the winter solstice have been re-vitalised in the last few years. During the communist regime, not a single word about Christmas was allowed to be mentioned, and it was less dangerous to celebrate Christmas at home in private.

Even at the time of suppression almost every family had a Christmas tree decorated with candles, tinsel and gingerbread cookies. A special Christmas dinner is prepared and the family has a reverent and quiet candle-lit meal. Towards the end of the evening there is a knock on the door and a bearded Father Christmas (Old Man Winter, as Latvians call him), arrives bringing a sack full of presents for all the good children – and adults!

Lithuania

The most important event of the Christmas season is the Christmas Eve supper – *Kucios*. It is the culmination of four weeks of fasting and preparation during Advent. Most of the food is traditionally dried, pickled or preserved. Kaleda Senis (Old Man Christmas) visits each house, delivering presents and accepting hospitality.

In great contrast to Christmas Eve, December 25th has always been a public celebration involving entire communities. Costumed revellers visit all the farmsteads and villages. In the country, people believed that New Year's night was miraculous. If, precisely at midnight, the sky was clear and full of stars, it would be a prosperous year. It was advisable on that night to pray before retiring or else nightmares would recur throughout the whole New Year.

Luxembourg

As more than 90 per cent of the population is Catholic, the majority of people regard Christmas as one of the most important festivals in the year, and they attend Midnight Mass on Christmas Eve.

Clubs and associations organise Christmas Eve and Christmas Day festivities. Some cities produce nativity plays with children as actors and others give concerts in the afternoon of December 25th. In some villages these concerts are followed by a Christmas Tree auction, the profits of which are given to charitable organisations. On Christmas Day there is the celebration of *Greiveldange* – the blessing of the wine. A procession of wine-growers carry a barrel of wine to the church where it is blessed. After the religious service, the barrel is put on tap and the wine tasted!

Macedonia

Customs that now take place are remnants of the past, although many have disappeared, and can only be traced by collectors of folklore. Christmas Eve was also known as Christmas Carol. This last named-celebration was connected with the returning of the sun from the south – for the birth of a new sun, in fact the renewal of life – crops, harvest and so on.

The main celebration has always been Christmas Eve, with a rich feast and a Christmas Carol fire, a leftover from the ritual fires lit in pagan times. There is also a Yule log burned on this night, and all members of the family keep vigil round this log, hence it is known as Awake Night.

Malta

Malta has had a long tradition of celebrating Christmas: Christianity has dominated the island since St Paul and St Luke were ship-wrecked there in 60 AD.

Christmas starts with home as well as church decoration, with the crib featuring heavily. The Maltese are quite house-proud and this is especially so in preparation for Christmas. Family homes are given an extra polish and Yuletide decorations put up. In the past thirty years the Christmas tree has featured in tandem with the more traditional crib. Christmas cards and gifts are exchanged, but in Malta this is done on a much smaller scale than in Northern Europe.

Monaco

At the centre of the ancient Principality of Monaco is to be found the Cathedral dedicated to St Nicholas, the saint at the very heart of the Christmas celebration in many European countries.

Up to the end of the last century, on Christmas Eve in Monaco all members of the family assembled to carry out the ceremony of the olive branch. Before sitting down to dine, the youngest or the oldest would dip an olive branch into a glass of old wine. He would then approach the fireplace, where a large fire of pine and laurel logs was burning, and with his branch make the sign of the cross while reciting some words extolling the virtues of the olive tree as the dispenser of benefits of all kinds. All those present would in turn wet their lips in the glass of wine, by way of an aperitif before the dinner.

Norway

Particularly in the country, preparations begin weeks before Christmas brewing the special Christmas beer. It is a jolly thought that an old Norwegian law required people to brew beer! This is followed by the traditional house-cleaning and the chopping of enough wood to keep the fires burning over the days of Christmas.

On Christmas Eve, the church bells start chiming to ring in the holiday. The Christmas celebration itself begins with the solemn reading of the Gospel, very likely from a family Bible that is several hundred years old. After this the family sits down to the traditional meal. Usually the main dish is porridge with a hidden almond, or where available fresh cod, or Lutefisk (see recipe page 110). The meal is followed by a ritual known as 'circling the Christmas tree'. Everyone joins hands to form a circle round the tree and then walks around it singing carols.

Poland

Almost 90 per cent of the population is Catholic, therefore most of the Christmas traditions have a connection with the Church holy days. The days of Advent are spent in preparation, including the thorough cleaning of the house, and observing the fast of no meat. The candles on the tree are never lit until the Christmas Eve supper, known as 'The Vigil'. The meal still does not begin until the first star appears in the sky – if it is cloudy, father says 'when'. The breaking and sharing of the bread wafers, known as Oplatek, is the the very esssence of Christmas Eve throughout Poland.

Gifts are brought to the children by Father Christmas on Christmas Eve, or by St Nicholas on December 6th. In one or two areas St Joseph does the honours, Joseph being a well-loved name in Poland.

Portugal

In the devout Northern provinces church services will be faithfully attended by everyone. The same applies to Madeira and the Azores. The remainder of the country may or may not rush to the Missa do Galo (Cockerel's Mass, the name given to Midnight Mass). Families get together on Christmas Eve to have supper and to exchange presents.

The Christmas tree and cards have been adopted, but traditions still very much centre around the dining table. The favourite nightcap on returning from Mass is hot chocolate and the fried cakes which are seasonal fare all over the country, exclusively made for the Christmas celebration. On Christmas Eve presents for children are left in their shoes or socks by the bottom of the bed, or around the fireplace. On New Year's Eve the sky is alight with spectacular fireworks, and the custom is to eat twelve raisins, one for each month of the New Year.

Romania

In December 1989, Romania was re-born as a nation, free to practise religion, and it is understandable that this comparatively new-found freedom has created a resurgence of national enthusiasm. Eighty-seven per cent of Romanians are Christians, with Catholics well represented.

As in so many European countries Christmas Eve is the main day of celebration, when presents are exchanged, and the main celebration meal is eaten. The Christmas tree is decorated with lit candles and the doors are then closed so that Baby Jesus can leave presents under the tree. They attend Mass on Christmas Eve and another service on the next day, December 25th, which is known as 'Second Day'.

Russia

The Russian Christmas, Rozhdestvo, falls on January 7th, following the 'Old Style' Julian Calendar instead of the 'New Style' Gregorian Calendar, brought in by Pope Gregory XIII in 1582. So, just when we are dismantling our Christmas decorations, the Russians are putting theirs up.

Traditions which had existed in the Tsar's Russia were forbidden by the Bolsheviks and many of them are now lost. In Socialist Russia New Year became the main holiday and Christmas was not celebrated. When the Iron Curtain came down, traditions from old Russia began to re-appear, and Christmas Day is again celebrated on January 7th, although New Year appears to be still the main celebration. It is at New Year that Father Frost (a Socialist, non-Christian invention) comes to deliver presents to the children.

San Marino

One of the smallest countries in the world, San Marino nestles right in the heart of Italy, proud of its independence. It is only natural, though, that most of its traditions are similar to the Italian ones, and this is certainly true of Christmas.

People spend the festive season getting together with family and friends to play 'tombola' or card games and eat dried fruit and nuts. As in Italy, the most important part of the season is Christmas Eve, when San Marinans respect the tradition of avoiding meat as a sign of fasting. Chick pea soup and 'baccalà' (salt cod) are often eaten that evening. At midnight the Baby Jesus is put in the manger of the *presepio* (crib).

Particular significance is attached to the traditional log, *il ceppo*, which burns during the Christmas period. It is said that the log has to burn every day because Baby Jesus goes there to warm himself. It also wishes good luck and long life to the head of the family, *il capofamiglia*. At the end of the season the log is completely burnt, but the ashes are kept because they keep storms away. A little bit of the ash has to be thrown as far away as possible to avoid nasty gossips, *le malelingue*!

Scotland

The celebration of Christmas in Scotland was very different before and after the Reformation. After the Reformation the celebration of Christmas was rather frowned upon. The church avoided anything which diverted attention from the worship of God, hence plain churches, unaccompanied singing etc. God was the centre of worship, not Jesus, and certainly not Mary.

It is only in the 20th century that Christmas has been celebrated in Scotland as extensively as in other European countries, and up to the 1950s Christmas Day was not even a holiday in Scotland. The holiday was the pagan festival of Hogmanay, New Year's Eve, and New Year's Day was the day off work. But gradually, English traditions have moved north, and now both Christmas and New Year are celebrated as holidays.

Slovakia

Slovakia lies at the meeting point of two European cultures – Western and Eastern. As in the West, Christmas in Slovakia is the occasion for family gatherings. In the past, families prepared for weeks in advance – there was the special cleaning throughout the house, baking to be done and decorations for the tree to be made. The main celebratory meal is on Christmas Eve, ending the long Advent fast.

These days, all through the countryside, processions of young people are much in evidence. These processions are characterised by funny costumes, singing, dancing and well-wishing. Children and young people put on fancy dress outfits and often wear masks. Popular Advent Day costumes are those of the mysterious St Lucy, the loveable St. Nicholas, savage-looking bears, somewhat gentler goats, or striking masks, made entirely of straw!

Slovenia

The Christmas period begins with Advent, continues to the Christmas Eve Feast and the Festival of the Three Kings, and is celebrated in many places until Candlemas (February 2nd). Because of the political situation in Slovenia until 1991, the majority of religious holidays, even Christmas, were observed mostly in the intimate family circle and there were no public religious holidays.

Arranging a crib is a very widespread custom and today these are found everywhere, in homes as well as in churches. The most common place to set up a crib is a corner of the main living room in the house, called 'God's Corner'. Putting up a decorated Christmas tree was still completely unknown in Slovenia in the middle of the 19th century. A remnant of the former custom of hanging a spruce instead lives on today in the custom of decorating the place with a rich spruce branch which is placed either behind the house crucifix or over the crib.

Spain

Christmas is a deeply religious holiday in Spain. The Christmas season officially begins on December 8th, the

The Origins of Father Christmas

Much of this chapter has been generously contributed by the Reverend David Lewthwaite.

In pre-Christian times presents were brought by the god Woden, or Odin, at the time of the great midwinter festival. The festival was held around December 25th and the God was said to ride across the skies on his eight-legged magic horse, or on a sledge pulled by reindeer, dispensing goodwill and presents to his faithful followers. These elements sound familiar. And there's more. Odin usually entered the house by the smoke hole, or chimney, in order to leave his gifts, as all the doors were shut to keep out the cold.

As Christianity became more powerful the church tried to stamp out pagan festivals, and one way it did this was to celebrate its own festivals at the same time. This happened in the case of the fertility goddess Oestre, whose feast became Easter, and in that of Old Year's Night which became Hallowe'en. Since no one knew for certain when Jesus was born, it was decided to celebrate his birth at the time of the midwinter festival in December, and so December 25th became Christmas Day. That's why holly, mistletoe and other evergreens, which were an important part of the old pagan festival, are still part of Christmas festivities today. In pagan times they symbolised the secret of life, since they stayed alive when all other plants seemed to die. In the case of the yule log, it is a leftover from the great fire which the pagans lit to keep the sun warm, so it would not die one cold winter's night.

That left the problem of Woden the gift-giver. A pagan God could hardly become part of a Christian festival. The witch doctors and shamans used to work themselves into a trance and then, filled with the spirit of Woden, they led the celebrations and gift-giving in their communities. This was a very popular part of the festivities and people were reluctant to let it go when they became Christian. The problem was solved by making St Nicholas the gift-giver.

St Nicholas was one of the most popular saints of the Middle Ages. He was adopted by many groups, but is remembered mainly as the Patron Saint of children. This is a detail from the Ansidei Madonna by the great Italian artist Raphael.

St Nicholas

Nicholas was the Bishop of Myra in Asia Minor. He was a rich man and it was his great delight to give his wealth away. Perhaps the best-known story is how he restored three boys to life. Nicholas entered an inn and found the innkeeper salting down the bodies of three boys he had just murdered. The bodies were in a tub, cut up ready to be sold for making pies. Nicholas said a blessing over the tub and the boys were restored to life. He is also said to have saved three young girls from being sold into slavery. The girls' father could not afford dowries for them so rather than getting married they were sold into slavery. Nicholas heard of their plight and threw three bags of gold into the house. One version of the legend says he threw the bags through an open window, but in another he threw the bags down the chimney and they fell into three stockings hanging up to dry. So we have another version of why gifts come down the chimney and why children hang up stockings on Christmas Eve.

It was because of stories like these that Nicholas was one of the most popular saints of the Middle Ages, and he is remembered mainly as the patron saint of boys and girls. In fact, there is an old Russian saying that 'if God were able to die, then St Nikolaus would have to become God'. In many European countries St Nicholas's Day, December 6th, is still a great festival and children put out their shoes on the windowsill for him to fill with sweets. In Belgium children put their shoes by the chimney, together with a saucer of carrots and turnips for the donkey. Sometimes children are encouraged to write down a list of presents they would like for Christmas on St Nicholas's Day. Nicholas carries these lists to Heaven and the gifts are sent by the Christ Child at Christmas.

Although the Scandinavian Julenisse and Tomte were traditionally dressed in red, blue-robed Santas were common in Britain and France in the nineteenth century.

In some countries St Nicholas has a stern companion, who checks to see if children have been naughty. In Luxembourg this person is called Black Peter and carries a stick. In Germany he is a dark-faced frightening character, known as Krampus or Pelzeback, who carries a bundle of switches with which to beat naughty children.

Early Dutch settlers in the USA took their traditions about St Nicholas with them, and the Dutch pronunciation of St Nicholas was soon corrupted into Santa Claus.

Father Christmas

In Britain and other Protestant countries there was less emphasis on saints and their festivals, including St Nicholas. Old Father Christmas has a long history in Britain and was a boisterous pagan character in mummers' plays for centuries. He became for many the personification of Christmas and its festivities. It was a

Joulupukki – Santa in Finland

Finland differs from most other countries in that Father Christmas really does visit people's homes on Christmas Eve. Usually he is just Father dressed up; sometimes another relative or a neighbour plays the part. The children of the family dress up as Father Christmas's helpers, in red tights, a long red cap and a grey cotton suit decorated with red. When Father Christmas arrives, he always asks the same question: 'Are there any good children here?' and the answer is an enthusiastic 'yes'.

The children sing to Father Christmas and there may even be time for a game. Then he tells them about the long journey he has made to see them, all the way from Korvatunturi, a fell in eastern Lapland. (A Finnish radio broadcast in 1927 announced that this was where Father Christmas lived, and he has made his headquarters there ever since.)

Because Christmas Eve is such a busy night for Father Christmas, he cannot afford to stay long in any one house. After one last song he tramps away into the snow, leaving behind a big basket of presents which his 'helpers' eagerly distribute.

Only after this important ceremony has taken place can the main Christmas meal be served.

tradition that somebody dressed as him and played a role in the festival much as the shaman did in the time of Woden. The Puritans tried to do away with him as they did with many festivities and customs but in Victorian times many of these traditions were revived, and amongst them Father Christmas.

There was little agreement as to the appearance of Father Christmas. In Estonia he is known as Old Man Yule, in Lithuania he is Kaleda Senis, dresssed in a white sheepskin coat and a tall sheepskin hat. In Norway and Sweden the

Father Christmas figure is a sprite, or house spirit, who lives under the floorboards of the house and looks after the family and their livestock. In Armenia it is midnight on New Year's Eve when Gakhand Baba (Father Christmas) knocks on the door carrying a huge bag of presents. Children are expected to sing a song or recite a poem before receiving the longed-for gift.

In many countries the belief remains that Christmas gifts come from the Christ Child, or from God. This is in fact very close to the earliest pagan belief that Woden gave the gifts, either in person or through helpers filled with his spirit. The older English tradition comes close to this in that Father Christmas is the personification of the spirit of Christmas. So we come full circle – in pagan tradition God gave the gifts, often through human mediums, and in Christian tradition God gave the gift of His son at Christmas. Gifts are given in memory of that first Christmas gift, and whether they come through the medium of parents, gnomes, Father Christmas, Santa Claus or whoever, Christians believe that the real Father of Christmas is God.

Samichlaus

Swiss customs and usages associated with Christmas have grown over the centuries out of a happy union of pagan elements, spirits and demons, and the Christmas tradition.

Heralding Christmas is Samichlaus (St Nicholas), who comes every December 6th to visit the children. In Catholic regions he appears in Episcopal robes, in Protestant communities as an old man wearing a dark Capuchin cloak. The children are told that he comes riding from afar out of the dim snowbound winter forest on a little donkey. He is the kindly, just herald of the Christ Child, and he comes laden with gifts. When the trembling children have recited the Versli (rhymes) especially learned for this occasion and the Chlaus has read out to them their list of sins of the past year and given them good advice, he opens up his heavy bag and there tumble out on the rug all kinds of sweetmeats, especially nuts and fruit, gingerbread and chocolate.

The big bag also serves the purpose of punishing bad children, since they can be stuffed into it and carried off into

---

SPECIAL TRADITIONS

The Julenisse and the Tomte

The belief in the Nisse (Norway) and the Tomte (Sweden) goes back to pagan times. According to old superstition, these house spirits guarded the land, people and animals in return for warmth and shelter, and a bowl of porridge on Christmas Eve. Today, they are also believed to be the distributors of the Christmas gifts.

The Nisse not only survives in Norwegian tradition but a strange intermingling has taken place between the Nordic Nisse and the St Nicholas of Central Europe, resulting in the strange mixture of gnome and bishop.

The most characteristic features of the Norwegian Julenisse are his red stocking cap and white beard. He wears knee breeches, hand-knitted stockings, a Norwegian sweater and a homespun jacket. He should be warm enough but on top he wears a heavy fur coat.

It is a wise move to make up a bed for the Nisse on December 24th and have the honorary place at the table standing ready and waiting for him. Make no mistake, the Julenisse is very real – but he does visit the homes with a sack of presents on Christmas Eve!

A Visit to Father Christmas

Judy Waples saw an advertisement for a Christmas-day trip to Lapland and answered it on a whim:

With three grandchildren aged seven, six and five, and a daughter-in-law who did not want to miss the event, we left Stansted early in the morning. Surprisingly there were more adults than children, but from the moment we got on the plane the day was tailor-made for children. The airline went out of their way to provide entertainment, carol singing, a Christmas supper, presents and crackers etc.

For Thomas to see the snow lying on the ground when we arrived at 1 p.m. in the dusk was pure magic. Bussed to the village, husky rides, reindeer rides, games in the snow, candlelit walks, learning about Lapland in a tipee (Granny bending double to get in!). The children did not wish to sample the reindeer milk that was on offer and were very concerned that we would all grow horns. The Laplanders were very friendly and hospitable and looked so colourful in their national costume.

The visit to Father Christmas was duly photographed and a dear little cow bell on a ribbon was their small gift. The whole village was lit by candles, the gift shops were full of local wooden toys and Christmas decorations. It was just a magical day and a memorable event for both children and adults.

Thank you for taking
Love from
Katie

Monday December 15th

Dear Granny

Thank you for taking me to Lapland. My best bit was the Huskydog ride. The ice slide was very very good, and I enjoyed meeting the real Santa Claus. I liked flying at night as well. It was a lovely Christmas present.

Love
from
Thomas

the forest. As a rule, however, this remains but a threat, which is readily resorted to by parents before Christmas as a disciplinary measure! St Nicholas is often accompanied by the Schmutzli (the Black One), a fearsome man in his dark mummer's guise with blackened face and hands. He clanks his heavy iron chain and also carries the switch, which St Nicholas leaves with the children. The custom of punishing and rewarding with gifts may already have been associated with the old demon's figure, otherwise, when the usage was Christianised, it would have hardly been likely for the practice to be attached to St Nicholas.

In some districts Samichlaus does not put in a personal appearance, but during the night throws his gifts in the door or through the window. He might also fill the shoes and boots left in front of the door or by the fireplace with gingerbread and nuts. Phantoms like to come and vanish again through the chimney. This is probably why they often appear with sooty hands and faces.

The Story of Christkindl

'Christkindl' is a German word used by children to refer to the Baby Jesus who brings gifts at Christmastime. It is also the name of a village in Austria. The following legend recounts the story of how the village came by its name.

Towards the end of the 17th century there lived in the town of Steyr a man named Ferdinand Sertl, who was the town organist and churchwarden, and who suffered from epilepsy. In 1695, Sertl received a wax statue of the Baby Jesus as a gift from the nearby convent. He took the statue into the woods, until he reached the place where the present-day village of Christkindl stands. There he carved out a hollow in the trunk of a fir tree and placed the statue inside. Every Sunday he returned to the spot to pray, and eventually he was cured of his illness. Word of the miracle soon got around, and people began to make pilgrimages to the statue for help in their afflictions.

Only two years later a hut was built around the fir tree. In 1703 Abbot Anselm of Garsten wrote to the Bishop of Passau that large numbers of pilgrims were visiting the 'Christkindl' and that it would be necessary to build a chapel there. The foundation stone of the present-day church was laid in 1708. Work began under the supervision of the baroque architect, Carlo Antonio Carlone and was completed under Jakob Prandtauer, who was probably the creator of the fine high altar with its carved angels. The focal point of the altar is the original tree-trunk with the statue of the Baby Jesus. Another notable feature of the altar is the tabernacle in the form of a globe with the continents shown in relief.

We owe much of our modern view of Santa Claus to the American poet Clement Clark Moore: his poem 'The Night Before Christmas' (1822) contains the lines 'His eyes – how they twinkled! His dimples how merry! His cheeks were like roses, his nose like a cherry!'

By the 20th century the village that grew up around the pilgrimage church had acquired the postal address 'Christkindl, Post Unterhimmel' (Post Office beneath Heaven). In 1950 a special post office was set up in the village during the Christmas season, with a specially designed stamp. The very first year brought an overwhelming response, with over 52,000 letters passing through the post office, and the next year it handled mail going abroad as well. Letters began arriving in Christkindl from all parts of Austria, for dispatch all over the world. The amount of mail being handled in Christkindl increased every year, and by the mid-fifties it had passed the half million mark. In the eighties the figure had risen to 1.8 million items of mail.

It goes without saying that children also address their Christmas wishes to Chriskindl Post Office. As long as the sender's address is legible, each child receives an answer from the Post Office.

A PERSONAL REMINISCENCE

Christmas and the Navy

Lady Holland-Martin DBE DL, former Chairman of the Board of Trustees of the NSPCC, has this recollection of a special appearance by Father Christmas:

In 1956 my husband as Flag Officer Flotillas took all the ships to Suez. I was left in Malta with the children and was told that they would not be back for Christmas, so I invited wives and children who were left behind to lunch. But the powers that be were wrong. The fleet sailed into Grand Harbour at 6.30 on Christmas morning. We were there. My husband had dressed up the Officer of the Watch at the prow of the ship as Father Christmas and the Marine band was playing 'Hark the Herald Angels Sing'. I was in tears.

Advent

Advent means arrival, and in many countries St Nicholas's Day (December 6th) is the beginning of Advent, the time of awaiting the birth of Christ. This is when children put out their shoes (either on the windowsill or outside the door) for sweets and other gifts. In some countries, such as Greece, it is a time of strict fasting, with December 5th and 6th as days of total abstinence. Little wonder that the Christmas feast is looked forward to with great anticipation! For those whose work involves helping other people prepare for Christmas, this is a very busy time, as Baroness Thatcher, whose father was a grocer, recalls:

'For many years we lived over the shop. So the run-up to Christmas was always one of the busiest times of the year. In addition to the usual Christmas trade, my father made up some 150 Christmas parcels under the auspices of the Rotary Club to distribute a few luxuries to families in need. And we all helped.

'Christmas Day was very traditional: church on Christmas morning followed by a large capon for Christmas dinner, which was always over in time to listen to the King's broadcast at 3 p.m.'

On Christmas Day 1932, King George V initiated the Monarch's Christmas Day message by means of the then-marvellous medium of radio, a tradition that has successfully made the transition to television and has been upheld ever since.

St Andrew

In Bulgaria St Andrew, whose festival day was November 30th, had to be appeased in many ways to ensure that he finally 'chased away the winter and the long nights'. On the eve of this special day, housewives would place grains and pulses into a pot to soak and swell, and would then boil them together on the following day; the family would usually first offer portions of the mixture to neighbours and then eat some themselves. In some districts it was only consumed within the family, to contain the good luck! Some of the grain might also be thrown to the hens or cattle to ensure a good dividend. Having feasted so well, people did not hasten to bed and after the ritual family gathering, groups of young men would form groups and choose a leader. Dressed in a holiday version of the national costume, wearing a large cloak, with their fur hats decorated with prunes or raisins or a wreath of greenery, and carrying a decorated stave, they would visit all the houses in the village to offer good wishes for the coming year. A few boys, known as the 'cats' would go ahead of the group and make loud meowing noises to announce their approach. One person, known as the 'donkey', carried the bags into which would go the gifts which were showered upon them. These *Kiledari* (carol singers) had a vast repertoire of songs which could suit everyone. The leader held a flask of wine – the singers would greet the head of the family, offer him a drink from the flask and if requested, would sing songs appropriate to the members of that family.

Advent Festivals

On the first Sunday in Advent, Danes prepare a crown made of spruce branches, decorated with four candles and red ribbons, which is hung from the ceiling. One candle is lit that first Sunday, then two the following Sunday, and so on. On that first Sunday in Advent family and friends gather to drink gløgg, or mulled red wine (see recipe page 164).

According to some traditions, we are linked to the ancient past by young wheat, which in the Advent period represents the awakening of all new life. It is still a custom in Slovenia, usually on St Lucia Day (December 13th) or St Barbara Day (December 4th), to plant wheat seeds in shallow bowls. The bowls are placed in the crib, under the Christmas tree, or elsewhere in the living room, and during the Christmas period fresh green wheat sprouts grow from the seeds. This wheat is left to grow until the Festival of the Three Kings (Epiphany) or until Candlemas (February 2nd) at the latest. Similar traditions still exist in France, where lentils are also grown, and in Croatia and the Ukraine, where the sprouted

A CHRISTMAS PROJECT

The First Advent Calendar

Around 100 years ago, a German mother attached 24 pieces of cake to a piece of cardboard – one to be eaten each day until Christmas – in order to keep her child occupied. By 1903 that child was the owner of a printing works in Munich and produced the first known Advent calendar with 24 windows, each with a small picture behind showing a child's wish, mostly toys.

German Advent calendars have become much more elaborate and nowadays calendars can be bought with a minuscule 'parcel' dangling on a thread from each of the 24 windows.

Make your own Advent calendar

1 Draw a suitable shape – a Christmas tree or the front of your house – on a large piece of card.

2 Mark 23 small windows and one larger one. Draw a picture over each window, or stick on pictures cut from old Christmas cards. Use angels, presents, robins, candles, stars, the stable, the shepherds or any other Christmassy theme you like. Traditionally, the big window should show the whole manger scene – Jesus, Mary and Joseph.

3 When all 24 pictures are in place, cut out 23 small pieces of paper and one large one, to fit the windows, and glue them over each picture like shutters, fastening them at the top only. Write a different number on each window, making the large one number 24.

4 Fix a piece of ribbon to the back with glue or tape and hang it up. Starting on December 1st, open a window every day until Christmas Eve, when you can reveal your final, big picture.

SPECIAL TRADITIONS

St Lucia

In Scandinavian countries the celebration of St Lucia's day, December 13th, is an important part of the run-up to Christmas itself. St Lucia is a young girl who according to tradition was martyred in Sicily at the time of the Emperor Diocletian. Some legends say she brought food to Christians hiding in the catacombs of Rome, wearing candles on her head to leave her hands free. The story was taken to Sweden by monks bringing the Gospel, and obviously struck a chord, for St Lucia's day is celebrated there with great enthusiasm, and the custom has spread to Norway and Finland. Every year Swedes celebrate 'The Queen of Light' – a national beauty contest where every town chooses its 'Lucia-bride'. On the early morning of December 13th in Swedish households, mother or daughter, niece or granddaughter is appointed to act the part of Lucia by wearing a simple white robe and a wreath of flickering candles on her head to awaken and offer morning coffee to sleeping parents, singing the ancient Lucia song.

St Lucia's Day is celebrated in Norway in schools, nursing homes, hospitals and day-care centres with processions led by a young Lucia in a white robe with a crown of lights on her head and a candle in her hand. In Norway, this night used to be called Lussinatten. It was the longest night of the year and no work was to be done. From that night until Christmas spirits, gnomes and trolls roamed the earth. Lussi, a feared enchantress, punished anyone who dared work. Legend also has it that animals talked to each other on Lussinatten, and that they were given additional feed on this longest night of the year.

Night plods with heavy tread,
court and cot cov'ring
O'er early, now sunshine's sped,
Shadows are hov'ring
Mirk in our home takes flight
When comes with tapers bright
Sancta Lucia, Sancta Lucia.

Mute was the night with gloom:
Now hear faint bustling
In ev'ry silent room,
Like pinions rustling.
Lo! on our threshold there
White-clad, with flame-crown'd hair
Sancta Lucia, Sancta Lucia.

Mirk soon swift wing shall take
From earth's vales darken'd
We to the words she spake
In wonder hearken'd.
Now shall another morn
From rosy skies be born.
Sancta Lucia, Sancta Lucia.

wheat has place of honour on the Christmas table.

This custom is much older than its Christian form, stretching back to the ancient civilizations in the East where shallow bowls of wheat were known as 'Adonis's Little Gardens'. They were named after the Greek god Adonis who represented the embodiment of plant growth. Adonis died each year with the wheat harvest and woke to new life with the young spring greenery after a period spent in the unknown land of death. Evidence of these 'little gardens' reaches back to the prophet Isaiah, and they are also documented in India in the third millennium BC. Today, of course, the meaning of this custom is quite unknown, as are its ancient roots. In some places, fortune-telling connected with the young wheat developed for the crops and even for the fate of the local people and the immediate family. However, these are only pale reminders of a past that was full of symbols of the awakening of new life.

Overleaf: **'The Census at Bethlehem' by Pieter Brueghel the Elder, showing a 16th-century Flemish interpretation of Christmas weather in the Holy Land!**

Christmas Eve

Some say, that ever 'gainst that season comes
Wherein our Saviour's birth is celebrated,
This bird of dawning singeth all night long;
And then, they say, no spirit can walk abroad;
The nights are wholesome; then no planets strike,
No fairy takes, nor witch hath power to charm,
So hallowed and so gracious is the time.
William Shakespeare

There is a widespread tradition of spring-cleaning the house on Christmas Eve, and in Lithuania this also involves changing the bed linen, bathing and putting on clean clothes, and settling all debts. This is often when the tree is put up. A colourful custom in Ireland was the lighting of a large, stout candle by the youngest member of the family, to be fixed in a prominent position on the inside windowsill, and smaller candles on all other sills, to be allowed to burn all night until the family left home in the morning for Mass in the local church. The traditional reason for the lighting of the candles was that the Holy Family might still be looking for shelter on such a night – or the light might guide some homeless wanderer to a welcome refuge. In Andorra too, many older folk still observe the custom of making sure the fire is burning and a chair placed nearby, in case the Mother of God chooses to drop in and warm herself at the hearth.

Christmas Eve at the turn of the last century, as depicted by Carlton Alfred Smith.

SPECIAL TRADITIONS

The Channel Islands

In the Channel Islands there are certain superstitions attached to Christmas Eve. In Jersey it is said that at midnight all water is turned to wine. Do not visit the well or you risk death. In Sark the superstition is that the water in the streams and wells turns into blood, and they also tell you that if you go and look you die within the year. One Sark man said that he was determined to go to the well and draw water at midnight, come what might. So on Christmas Eve he went out to the well in his back yard. As he crossed the threshold he tripped and hit his head against the lintel of the door, and was picked up unconscious the next morning. Most people would have taken this as a warning and desisted, but he was obstinate, and the following Christmas Eve he left the house at midnight as before, but as he approached the well he heard a voice saying :

> Qui veut voir
> Veut sa mort.

Then at last he was frightened and rushed back into the house, and never again did he attempt to pry into forbidden mysteries.

In Jersey after the Reformation it was ordered that all church bells, except for one in each parish, should be collected and sold to raise funds for the erection of new fortifications. The bells were taken down and loaded onto a ship which sank outside the harbour, giving rise to a local superstition that they could be heard ringing under water whenever a gale was due, tolling a knell for drowned seamen.

There were no Christmas services during the Calvinist regime, and the custom arose in three of the parishes of ringing the sole surviving bell for 36 hours without stopping, from noon on Christmas Eve until midnight on Christmas Day. For the lads of the parish, this was a party, enlivened by much home-brewed cider. This practice continued in St Mary's parish even when Christmas Day services were resumed, though it was impossible for the Rector to make himself heard above the cacophony.

Many Rectors tried unsuccessfully to stop the practice. Then came a young Rector, the Rev Le Couteur Balleine, who was determined to hold a Christmas service in peace and quiet. On Christmas Eve, 1858, he fitted new locks to the church doors, removed the bell-rope and clapper and the belfry ladder. But the parishioners broke the locks and threw the doors into the rectory garden. One fetched a ladder, another galloped to St. Helier to buy a new rope while others woke the blacksmith and worked his bellows while he forged a new clapper. The bell rang as usual for the whole of that Christmas Day and the Parish Assembly subsequently asserted: 'If there was any disturbance, it was due to the pig-headed behaviour of the Rector.'

The custom has since been modified. The bell is rung from noon on Christmas Eve until 11.30 p.m., then the belfry door is locked until after morning services on Christmas Day. After that until midnight, the bell-rope is again available to all comers. The consumption of cider by the ringers is slightly less than in the past.

In the Channel Islands it is considered unlucky to enter the cow stall or shed in case cattle are kneeling ready for midnight obeisance to the Infant Jesus. In Belgium it was believed that the sheep all turn round to face the east, the cows kneel down in the straw, and the bees swarm out and hum. Wiltshire folklore said that the owners of hives had to rouse them on Christmas morning with a gentle knock, and the message 'Christ is Born'. If they failed to do this, the bees would not be ready when the time came to start their year's garnering.

In Slovenia people were convinced that Heaven opened on this night, that wine flowed in the streams, that water changed into silver and gold, and that even animals could speak. The belief that animals could speak on Christmas Eve was generally held throughout Europe.

In Finland and Estonia the President declares Christmas Peace, a tradition which began in the 17th century by order of Queen Kristina of Sweden.

In Malta at the beginning of Advent a young boy – or often girl these days – is chosen in each parish and coached in the art of narrating the story of the nativity from the church pulpit during the service on Christmas Eve. Families consider it an honour for one of their children to be chosen; indeed, they help the child as he/she commits to memory a ten-minute long oration. Once over, the child is presented with a suitable memento by the local parish priest.

Some societies take special precautions against evil at this time. In Croatia the men used to fire off various weapons such as muskets and rifles, now they use revolvers and automatic weapons – noise and gunshots are a ritual for driving away

A traditional children's street procession in Malta. An image of the Infant Jesus leads the parade.

usually nougats and chocolates – under the blanket. The children are then encouraged to beat the log with a stick while singing some traditional ditty. The custom is said to have its origin in pre-Christian rites. The Tió represents nature, dormant through the winter months, but now summoned to life (symbolised by the singing and striking with the stick) and producing its fruit again at the end of the winter solstice.

Seasonal shop window decorations in Germany.

evil. As a protection from witches, on Christmas Eve a cross has to be drawn with garlic on all the doors of the house and the stable and cellar, and that clove of garlic is then pressed into the keyholes so that witches cannot enter! In Slovakia, garlic and onion is used in the cooking as a protection against evil. In Macedonia every housewife used to prepare a pie on Christmas Eve with a silver coin hidden inside it. The host would divide up the pie, reserving a piece for God and the house. The person who found the coin put it in a glass of water from which everyone drank, for good health and joy.

The Andorran Tió

The Tió is a Christmas Eve custom popular with youngsters in Andorra. Parents place an oak log near the main fireplace and cover it with a blanket. A few moments later, while the children's attention is distracted, they slip small presents –

First Footing

In some countries the tradition of first-footing – the ritual exchange of presents with the first person across the threshold after midnight – takes place at Christmas rather than New Year. The person is either lucky or unlucky, and a dark man is usually preferred. In Yugoslavia, the first-footer brings corn, which is scattered over the threshold while saying 'Christ is born'. The head of the household says, 'He is born indeed' and

The Icelandic Yuletime Lads

Celebrations start in Iceland at 6 p.m. precisely on Christmas Eve – Yule Eve. This may have descended from the old days when a new day began not at midnight, but at 6 p.m. Thus in Iceland there are thirteen rather than twelve days of the Yuletide season. This country has many traditional stories and much seasonal folklore, the best known being the Jólasveinarnir or the Yuletime lads and their terrible parents, Gryla and husband Leppalüdj. The belief was that Gryla stole children who had been naughty during the year. The Jólasveinarnir live in the mountains, and they start to arrive in town, one a day, thirteen days before Christmas Eve, with the last one arriving on that very morning. They leave little presents for the children in shoes placed on the windowsill. If the children have been naughty they are left a potato! The lads start returning for the mountains on Christmas Day. At first the clothing of the Jólasveinarnir was just the ordinary everyday wear of the Icelander, but this century, they have taken to wearing the traditional red of St. Nicholas or Santa Claus.

sprinkles the first-footer with corn in return. This ritual ends with the first-footer hitting the Yule log to make sure the sparks fly, and sometimes placing a gift of money or fruit on the log.

The Christmas Eve Feast

In many European countries the main Christmas meal is on Christmas Eve, not Christmas Day, and sometimes follows attendance at Midnight Mass. In Catholic countries the period from Advent to Christmas Eve is one of fasting, and the Christmas Eve meal therefore contains no meat. Many countries have a tradition of eating fish at the Christmas Eve meal, for example salt cod in Portugal and Sweden, eels in Italy, fried fish in Gibraltar, carp in Poland and Slovakia. Twelve or thirteen dishes are often served, to commemorate the Last Supper. In Provence there are thirteen desserts, mostly dried fruits and nuts. In some central European countries the signal for the meal to begin is when the first evening star appears. If the sky is cloudy, the man of the house decides when it is time to eat. Sometimes the meal begins with the ritual breaking and sharing of the bread wafers, symbolising the communion of all Christians. In Lithuania a small plate, with as many wafers as people present, is placed in the centre of the table – in some regions they used to be called God's cakes. There are greetings and good wishes to everyone and the exchange of pieces of wafer, symbolising the sharing of daily bread with others.

There is another delightful tradition in Lithuania. If a family member has died during the past year or cannot attend the Christmas Eve meal, an empty place is left at the table, on which a plate is placed and a chair drawn up, but no spoons, knives or forks are set. A small candle is placed on the plate and lit during the meal. It is believed that the spirit of the absent family member participates along with everyone else. At the end of the meal, the food is not cleared away, so that the souls of dead members of the family can gather around it during the night. In Macedonia left-over food remained on the table overnight for Father Christmas to share the meal. In the area of Kukush, dinner was actually cooked for Father Christmas and set in the yard while the host would say 'Welcome, Father Christmas – let us dine.'

After the meal is traditionally the time for gathering round the fire and fortune-telling. In Lithuania people pull straws from under the tablecloth – a long stem means a long life, and a short one means that you might not live to the next Christmas. In Bulgaria, twelve flakes of onion were laid out, representing the months of the coming year and a little salt was put on each. According to whether the salt became moist or remained dry they could forecast the weather, and the harvest was judged by how the fire was burning. Personal fortunes and other tokens were told by the finding of a lucky coin concealed in the special loaf of bread. In Poland, girls would blindfold each other and touch the fence pickets on their way to Midnight Mass. Touching a straight, smooth picket would forecast a resourceful husband, while a crooked, rough

one was an indication that the girl would find a clumsy, awkward spouse!

In Croatia the long Christmas Eve evening before going to Mass was full of laughter and entertainment. While people sipped their wine, the funny little story of the woman from Carniola was often recounted. They say that at the time of the Christmas Vigil, this Kranjica, before going to church, went to a tavern and ordered a glass of rakija. She dunked her bread in the drink, ate it and followed this by downing the rakija. Then she said, 'The bread drank one glass, now I'll have one.' When she had gulped down one more shot, she went on her way to the church, completely tipsy from the rakija. The world spun about her – even the altars whirled around her. And then she said, 'Mother of God, I came to walk about you, but you are walking around me, but it doesn't matter! I am Mary, you are Mary, I am a mother – you are a mother. They nailed your son to the cross – they hanged mine, so we are equal!'

Incense

At nightfall in Slovenia on Christmas Eve the custom continues today of burning incense and sprinkling the house and the other farm buildings with holy water. The custom is widespread in the countryside and in the towns where even large apartment blocks and whole neighborhoods smell sweetly of incense. The incense is placed on a brazier that is carried through all the rooms in the house. The other farm buildings, meadows, orchards and vineyards are also incensed and sprinkled with holy water. Before incense purchased at the church or in specialized stores came into use, branches from the blessed Palm Sunday butaricas (sheaves of spring greenery) that had been saved in the attic were placed on the brazier. Incensing and sprinkling the home is accompanied with prayers as the whole family moves in a procession from one room to the next.

What Made the Holy Child Smile

This charming piece is by Karl Heinrich Waggerl.

When Joseph and Mary were on their way from Nazareth, the Archangel Gabriel secretly came down from Heaven just to check that all was as it should be in the stable. It was hard to understand why the Lord had to be born in a poor miserable stable and why his cradle had to be a manger. But the least Gabriel wanted to do was to instruct the winds not to whistle through the cracks too harshly, and to make sure the clouds would not dissolve with emotion and flood the child with their tears, and the light in the lantern had to be told once again to shine modestly and not to blink and sparkle like a Christmas star.

At the same time, the Archangel got rid of all the small animals in the stable, the ants and spiders and mice, for it was unthinkable what might happen if Mother Mary were to be frightened by a mouse before her time! Only the ass and the ox were allowed to stay – the ass because it would be useful later on for the flight to Egypt, and the ox because it was so big and lazy that all the hosts of angels would not have been able to shift it anyway.

Finally, Gabriel scattered a crowd of little angels over the stable rafters – the tiny variety that consists mainly of heads and wings. They were, after all, only intended to sit there and watch and to report immediately if anything threatened the child in its bare poverty. One more look round, and the mighty one unfolded his wings and took off.

So all was well. But not all that well, because there was a flea still asleep in the straw at the bottom of the manger. This tiny horror had escaped the Archangel Gabriel, for what would an Archangel have to do with fleas?

When the miracle had happened and the child was lying there on the straw in all its loveliness and touching poverty, the little angels on the rafters under the roof could contain themselves no longer, and in their delight they flew around the manger like a flock of doves. Some of them fanned the boy with balmy fragrances, while others tugged at the straw and smoothed it so that not a stalk could press on him or pinch him.

All this buzzing around woke up the flea in the straw. It was terrified because it thought somebody was chasing it, as usual. It hopped around the manger and at last, in utter desperation, it slipped into the Christ Child's ear.

'Forgive me,' the flea whispered breathlessly, 'but I can't help it. They will kill me if they catch me. I'll soon be off again in a second, your Holiness. Just let me find a way.' It looked around and soon thought of a plan. 'Listen,' it said, 'if I gather up all my strength, and if you keep still, I could reach the bald head of Joseph, and from there I could make the window bars and the door.'

The Adoration of the Shepherds, as portrayed by Rembrandt in the 17th century.

'Go on then, jump!' said little Jesus inaudibly. 'I will keep still!' And the flea jumped. But it was inevitable that it tickled the child a bit when it got into position and drew its legs up under its belly.

At that moment the Holy Mother started to shake her sleeping husband. 'Just look!' said Mary happily, 'He is smiling already!'

St Stephen's Day (Boxing Day)

In Wales, a somewhat barbaric practice on St Stephen's Day – December 26th – involved holly-beating the bare arms and legs of female servants until the blood flowed. This derived from the practice of bleeding animals on this day to improve their health and stamina. Whether the serving girls felt similarly invigorated is debatable.

On the Isle of Man the highlight of St Stephen's Day (otherwise known as Boxing Day) has for generations been Hunt the Wren, a very old custom whose origins are shrouded in the mists of time. Originally it was quite a bloodthirsty ritual, as gangs of youths would scour the countryside looking for a defenceless wren to trap and kill, but now a more humane option is to use an artificial bird. The wren is the centrepiece for a 'bush': two wooden hoops set at right angles and placed on top of a pole and covered with ribbons and evergreens. The 'bush' is then carried from house to house while the group sing the 'Hunt the Wren' song and hope to collect some money or treats for their troubles. The song charts the progress of the poor wren from being hunted, caught, cooked and then eaten. There are many suggestions as to why the poor wren should be singled out for such treatment, such as it being a commemoration of the martyrdom of St Stephen or revenge on the wren because it is the re-incarnation of an enchantress who lured men to their death by drowning. The feathers of the wren are distributed amongst the 'wren' boys as a good luck charm, being particularly potent against witchcraft and to prevent a shipwreck (an important concern for Manx fishermen).

St Stephen is the protector of horses and livestock in general. In a special ritual in Dolenjska, Slovenia, local people ride horses to the church, where the priest blesses them. In central Slovenia, especially in the area between Skofja Loka, Kranj and Kamnik, wooden figures of horses, cattle and pigs are brought to the church for blessing on St Stephen's Day, symbolically praying in this way for their health and growth. Along with the figures, which the parish clerk collects after the blessing and keeps until the following year, people also bring bags of salt and wheat to the blessing, taking them home after the ceremony in the church to feed to their animals. Because the figures of horses and other domestic animals have been kept in this way every year, some churches in this region have genuine galleries of 19th-century Slovene folk art. As a matter of interest, figures of horses are still brought for blessing to St Stephen's church in Ljubljana, in a part of the city where there are no longer any horses and which is otherwise developing into a modern urban area.

St Stephen's Day in Slovenia: figures of horses are brought to the altar to be blessed.

New Year

Heralding the new year is a much older tradition than Christmas, and almost every country has its own celebrations. In some countries New Year was until recently the more important event. In Scotland, for example, until fairly recently Christmas Day was not even a public holiday, while New Year definitely was – and is. In Scotland as in many countries there is a tradition of spring-cleaning the house (it is particularly important that the hearth is clean and swept) and also of 'first-footing'. It is important that the first person across the threshold after midnight carries gifts to bring luck and prosperity to the house (a tall dark man is traditionally preferred). In Armenia It is still the tradition for the

'Mr Punch goes first-footing' – a cartoon from *Punch's Almanack*, 1897.

man of the house or a relative to be the first visitor to knock and enter after the visit of Gakhand Baba, to ensure that no one could possibly bring bad luck for the rest of the year.

In Socialist Russia, New Year became the main holiday. When the Iron Curtain was removed, some of the old traditions came back and Christmas Day has returned, although New Year appears to be the greater celebration. It is on New Year's Eve that a gaily decorated fir tree is carried indoors – after the traditional cleaning of the house. The Russians celebrate until daylight, and then, if the frost is not too severe, many people carry the carnival spirit out-of-doors, making for the squares and parks, colourful with huge lighted fir trees. Here, to the irresistible beat of the music, the high-spirited Russians dissolve into song and dance.

In Switzerland, the Chlause (St Nicholas figures) appear not only on December 6th but also at New Year. The Chlause of Urnasch in the Canton of Appenzell Ausserrhoden come out on January 13th. According to the Julian Calendar the New Year falls on this date. There are two kinds of Chlause. One embodies beneficent spirits. Their immense cowls and hats are adorned with thousands of beads and other trinkets and they carry entire Alpine scenes on their head-dresses. The wild Chlause, on the other hand, are demons in animal and human form. They are enveloped in shaggy costumes of skins and brushwood, and wear fearsome masks. The Chlause proceed from farm to farm, delighting people with their dances and Zauerli (a form of yodelling native to Appenzell), for which they receive gifts.

There are special water ceremonies associated with New Year. In Greece the 'Renewal of Waters' takes place – all water jugs in the house are emptied and refilled with the new St Basil's water celebrating the New Year. In the past, this ceremony was accompanied by offerings to the naiads, spirits of springs and

SPECIAL TRADITIONS

The Welsh Mari Lwyd

One of the most famous emblems of the season in Wales is the remarkable and colourful Mari Lwyd. Its main element is the skull of a horse bedecked with ribbons attached to a pole and draped with a billowing sheet. Beneath the sheet someone activates the snapping jaws of the beast. Gruesome as it appears, this apparition is welcomed. Mari Lwyd prances into the house ahead of his followers, paying special attention to the women folk, nudging, blowing and pretending to bite them. Having sung for a while, this invader is given food and drink before departing with a blessing on the house.

Mari Lwyd means Grey Mare, but was Christianised to become associated with the Virgin Mary and then translated as 'Grey Mary'. She is often associated with the Rhiannon of Welsh legend, or even with Epona, the ancient Celtic horse deity. Whatever her lineage, she is still welcomed every New Year's Eve in the public houses of Glamorgan!

Mari Lwyd as it is practised today (left) and in 1910 (right).

fountains. In South Wales, crowds of boys used to visit local houses early on New Year's morning, carrying a vessel of cold spring water freshly drawn. They also carried twigs of box, holly, myrtle and rosemary. The hands and faces of everyone they met on their rounds were sprinkled with water. In every house they entered, they sprinkled each room with New Year's Water and, given the chance, the residents, who would often still be in bed!

In Finland, on the other hand, the sauna is an integral part of the New Year. Travelling around the Finnish countryside on New Year's Eve smoke will be rising from almost every sauna-house.

New Year's Eve has always prompted fortune-telling. In Estonia girls find out about their marriage prospects with the help of a shoe. Standing with her back to the door, each girl throws her shoe over her shoulder. If the shoe lands with the toe pointing to the door, she will be a bride during the oncoming year. But if the heel points to the door, there is no hope for at least twelve months! In Cyprus on the Eve of St Basil (New Year's Eve), the

family would gather round a terracotta brazier to tell friends' fortunes with olive leaves. The custom was to take an olive leaf and make the Sign of the Cross over the fire, reciting special verses to St Basil, then toss it into the brazier. If the leaf jumped out of the fire, the house was filled with shouts of joy, but if the leaf burnt without moving, there were cries of despair. In Vienna, lead is heated in a spoon over a candle, then poured into cold water. The resulting shapes are held between the candle and a wall, and the shadow cast is said to reveal the future.

On the Isle of Man, fortune-telling rituals related to trying to discover who might die during the year. A thimbleful of salt was laid out on a plate for each member of the household or an ivy leaf was put into water. If a pile of salt collapsed or a leaf withered overnight, someone would die. Ashes from the fire would be raked over the floor last thing at night and in the morning checked for fairy footprints. If any trace were found, the direction of the footprints was critical; toes to the door would

SPECIAL TRADITIONS

Orkney

The Ba' Game (above) is played in the streets of Kirkwall every Christmas and New Year's Day. The game has been played in its present form since 1850, but undoubtedly ball games have been played for a very long time. There are records from Greek and Roman times of ball games being played and mass-football seems to have been played in Roman-occupied Britain. It is only now played in a few towns in Scotland and England such as Jedburgh, Ashbourne and Workington. In Kirkwall the two sides are 'Uppies' and 'Downies'. The Ba' is thrown up at 1 p.m. on Kirk green opposite the cathedral by some public figure, with up to 200 players eagerly awaiting the chime of the bells. The Downies' goal is the sea, within the basin of the harbour. The Uppies must go round Mackinson's Corner, opposite the Catholic Church.

The town takes on the appearance of siege during the period of the Ba', with shutters and barricades on all the shops and houses on possible Ba' routes – cars come near at their peril while young children and elderly people are well-advised to keep clear.

SPECIAL TRADITIONS

The Magic of Yule

In Iceland the night of the year when the old year changes into the new is regarded as magical. This is the eighth night of Yule, when cows can gain human speech and seals take on human form, the dead rise from their graves, and the Elves move house! A traditional greeting to the elves was:

> Let those who want to, arrive,
> Let those who want to, leave
> Let those who want to, stay
> Without harm to me or mine.

indicate someone would die; heel to the door and the family could expect a new addition. Extra care then needed to be exercised in sweeping the floor so that everything went into the hearth and good luck was not swept out of the house.

Epiphany (Twelfth Night)

In Italy and Andorra, the main exchange of gifts takes place on January 6th, the feast of Epiphany, the celebration of the Magi's visit to the Christ Child.

In Italy and Sicily, children anxiously await a visit from La Befana, who brings gifts for the good — and punishment for the bad. La Befana was asked to accompany the Wise Men, but declined because she was too busy cleaning her home — an obsession with this old woman. The Wise Men left without her, she promising to catch up with them when she had finished her cleaning. By the time she was ready, the Wise Men were far away. She frantically started to run after them with her gifts for the Christ Child, still carrying her broom. Magically, she began to fly on her broomstick but could not find the Wise Men or the Christ Child. Instead, she leaves gifts for other children — treats for those who are good, coal for those who are not so good — but actually every child receives a piece of coal as well as the present, because we could all do better.

Epiphany marked the end of Christmas festivities in Wales. There was a strange custom on this day in Glamorganshire where cakes were specially baked for the occasion. The old people who clung to ancient customs, used to divide the cake in a figurative sense between Christ, the Virgin Mary, the Magi and the company.

On the Isle of Man Twelfth Night festivities usually took place at the public house, and included prophesies of whom each maid should marry. The fiddler would lay his head in each young lady's lap and would be asked in turn whom each maid would marry. Each answer would be accepted solemnly as the oracle (rather than as the fiddler's educated guess or his own personal whim). Although a source of great merriment, it could also be a source of tears and vexation for 'couples' with strong aversions, which probably caused more merriment to the others. Valentines or legards would be appointed in turn to all the men and then a supper followed where each man paid for his legard. A *laare vane* or 'white mare' (a wooden horse's head with a white sheet to cover the wearer) would join the party and badger and harass the guests until finally chased from the room amongst much rough and tumble.

Right **A 16th-century Adoration of the Magi by Marcellus Coffermans.**

Holly, Ivy and Mistletoe

Green boughs, holly, ivy and mistletoe were all used in the pagan midwinter celebrations long before the advent of Christmas. They were a symbol that life would return to the forest, and were venerated as such.

Mistletoe was prized by the Celtic druids as a sacred, healing plant which also warded off evil. No one but a druid using a gold sickle was permitted to gather the plant and the severed sprigs were caught in a white cloth before they touched the ground. Two white bulls would then be sacrificed. It was a symbolic ceremony, reflecting the mythical tale of the priest-king being killed by a younger and stronger successor.

Norse mythology also contains a powerful story about mistletoe. The goddess Frigg had made all living things promise not to harm her favourite son, Baldur, but had forgotten the lowly mistletoe, which the jealous god Loki was able to use to

Above and opposite, Christmas arrangements of holly, ivy and mistletoe.

inflict a deadly wound. All the creatures on Earth wept at the death of Baldur. Their tears were placed on the mistletoe, and transformed into creamy, pearl-like berries, ridding the plant of its fatal tendencies. From this story springs the belief that kissing under a sprig of mistletoe brings luck all year long.

An interesting footnote to these myths is that the ancients cut mistletoe on Midsummer's Eve. It was linked to Christmas only because this was the time when the plant was pruned.

As with other symbols of our pagan past, the use of evergreens was adopted by the Christian church, except for mistletoe, whose symbolism was considered too potent. Holly was acceptable, as its red berries could be said to symbolise Christ's blood, but mistletoe has always been banned in churches.

Remnants of earlier beliefs lingered on in countries such as Croatia where houses were decorated with bunches of sage, and bunches of ivy were fixed on doors and windows to keep the witches away. People would bring to church armfuls of maple, ivy and olive branches, also a cloth holding salt and a jug of water, and the priest would bless each branch, dip his hand into the water, make a Sign of the Cross and throw a little salt on it.

SPECIAL TRADITIONS

The Glastonbury Thorn

This extract comes from The Christmas Almanac *by Michael Stephenson:*

The old abbey at Glastonbury in Somerset is now only a ruin, but for many hundreds of years it has been used as a holy place. The site of King Arthur's Camelot is said to be nearby and some say Arthur and his queen, Guinevere, are buried in the abbey grounds. Even today the ruins have a magical atmosphere.

An old legend tells of the time when Glastonbury was visited by Joseph of Arimathea; Joseph had been close to Jesus and it was in Joseph's family tomb that the body of Christ was laid after the crucifixion. The legend related how the apostle Philip sent Joseph to England in AD63 to found the first Christian settlement, at Glastonbury. Joseph is supposed to have brought with him the Holy Grail, the cup from which Jesus had drunk at the Last Supper with the disciples. When Joseph arrived at Glastonbury, he is said to have plunged his walking staff, made from hawthorn, a very hard wood, into the soil. The staff took root and a hawthorn bush grew from it. Every Christmas the bush flowers in memory of Jesus' birth.

In 1900 a cutting from the legendary thorn bush at Glastonbury was given to St Albans School in Washington DC. It first flowered in 1918 and then every Christmas since.

Flowers

British gardening writer Ursula Buchan has contributed this lovely piece about the Christmas Rose:

Thanks to one much-loved carol we in Great Britain are inclined to think of the holly and ivy as being the Christmas plants par excellence, but it would be a mistake to think that these are the only plants which have something to offer at Christmastime. For in a mild year, even in a small garden, there can easily be twenty different kinds of flowers to pick on Christmas day, and a great many more berries, seedheads and coloured foliage.

Of all the flowers associated with this season, the so-called Christmas rose, *Helleborus niger*, must be the most evocative. It finds its way on to Christmas wrapping paper, Christmas cards, silk flowers and candle decorations. The combination of pure white, open-cupped flowers and dark green foliage seems particularly appropriate for the season, although it must be said that it is a fortunate and favoured garden which sees the

The Christmas rose (below) **and the passionflower** (opposite).

flowers fully expanded by Christmas Day. They are more likely to flower after the New Year. The flowers are round, single, up to 7cm/3in across, and carried singly on sturdy stems. The leaves are evergreen, leathery, and divided into seven or nine segments, usually. There are many different varieties on the market, not all of them rightly named; one of the best, because of the larger size of the flowers, is 'Potter's Wheel', with blooms up to 12cm/5in across. This was raised in the 1950s. Since then, a number of other garden worthy varieties have been bred, notably 'Blackthorn Strain' and 'White Magic'.

Helleborus niger is not straightforward to grow. It is native to the mountains of central Europe and demands limey soil, which is not too heavy, but does not dry out in summer, preferably enriched with leaf-mould. It is best planted in dappled shade, such as is found underneath deciduous trees.

Passionflower

The legend that this plant of the genus *passiflora* resembles in its parts the instruments of the Crucifixion seems to have arisen in Spain. The resemblances are said to be as follows:

The leaf symbolises the spear
The five anthers – the five wounds of Christ
The tendrils – the cords or whips
The column of the ovary – the pillar of the cross
The stamens – the hammers
The three styles represent the three nails
The fleshy threads inside the flowers – the crown of thorns
The calyx – the glory
The white tint – purity
The blue tint – heaven
It keeps open three days, symbolising the three years' ministry of Christ.

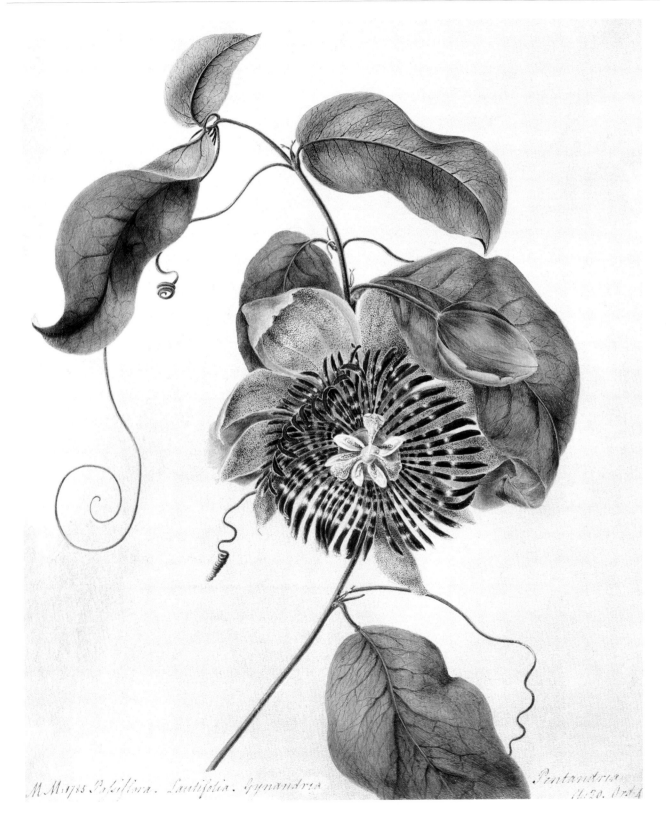

M.M.1783.Passiflora. Lautifolia. Gynandria.   Pentandria.
                                                               ??.20. Ord 4

Trees and Logs

Tree worship dates back to prehistoric times, and the evergreen was particularly venerated at the time of the midwinter solstice as being the only tree in the forest with the promise of survival to spring. Small green trees might be brought indoors at midwinter to symbolise fertility.

The Christmas tree as we know it today seems to have had its origin in Germany. In the Middle Ages, there were mystery plays each December 24th, the feast day of Adam and Eve. The plays invariably featured a decorated evergreen which represented the Tree of Life from which Adam and Eve ate, and as a result were banished from the Garden of Eden. Over the

Citrus slices, terracotta and straw figures make cheerful tree decorations (left)**, while colourful ribbons and traditional Christmas plants bring a festive feel to the simplest furniture** (above)**.**

centuries, the plays strayed from their religious origin and the Church ceased to sponsor them, but people continued to set up and decorate a tree in their homes every Christmas.

From Germany the tree custom spread to other countries, the tree being decorated with apples, paper flowers and candles. There is a legend in Germany that Martin Luther, while walking home through the woods one Christmas Eve, was struck by the beauty of the stars glittering through the branches of the firs, and set up for his children a tree lit with countless candles, as a symbol of the starry heavens whence the Christ Child had descended to earth. In Bulgaria the tree was either fruit-bearing or known for its resistance, such as pear or a three-year-old oak. It was important that during the felling the chosen tree did not rest on the ground. In some districts the feller would carry the tree home and into the house saying, 'I am home and God is with me' and the family would respond 'Amen, God grant it be so.'

In Croatia, before the Christmas tree was generally accepted, it was the Christmas branch, broken off some fruit tree as early as St Lucia's Day (December 13th) and put into water so that it would flower by Christmas Eve. Figures of dough would be hung on it. In Russia cherry boughs were similarly cut on St Catherine's Day (December 7th) and kept in water. On Christmas morning they would then be arranged in front of the icons.

Christmas trees are also not a tradition in Yugoslavia, where small oak branches are brought into the house. Twigs bearing acorns are placed on the dinner table to symbolise prosperity. After the festival, the branches are burned in the fire – a remnant of the ancient pagan tradition of the midwinter fires. Christmas trees only became popular in Poland at the end of the 19th century. Earlier than that a freshly-cut spruce top would hang from the ceiling to bring luck. This would be suspended in God's Corner or the Holy Corner, facing east. In Spain, Italy, France and other Catholic countries the nativity scene or crib has always been the focal point in the home, rather than the tree, though in recent years the tree has appeared as well.

Christmas trees were introduced to Britain in the 19th century by Prince Albert, the German husband of Queen Victoria. From Germany too came the now traditional spun glass

'Bringing home the Yule faggots' – from a 19th-century children's book.

decorations. In 1880 glass-makers in Thuringia discovered how to blow glass balls and bells, which are now used to trim Christmas trees all over the world. In Lithuania however, each family makes and collects straw ornaments for the tree. These are used year after year, and courses on how to make these ornaments are offered every year before Christmas.

Most trees are lit with artificial fairy lights, but in Germany and Austria there is still a tradition of lighting candles on the tree. In Durbuy, a tiny Belgian town, small candle-lit trees line the streets at Christmas.

In Britain the tree is often put up and decorated days, sometimes weeks, before Christmas, but in most European countries the tree is only put up on Christmas Eve. The tree is decorated, and then the living-room door is locked so that the Christ Child can bring the presents. Carols are still sung round the tree in some places before the presents are opened. In Sweden the tradition is to join hands and walk around the tree singing 'Thou green and glittering tree – Hello!'

In Holland Christmas is a short holdiay, and the Christmas tree is dismantled on December 26th and left outdoors – children then add it to all the others on the Christmas bonfires.

The Yule Log

The Yule log is a much older tradition than the Christmas tree, and like so many Christmas customs has its origins in pagan fertililty rites. Today most people think of a delicious chocolate cake shaped like a log (see recipe page 140), but originally the Yule log was ceremonially dragged home from the woods and lit

The Christmas Tree in Trafalgar Square

The Christmas tree in Trafalgar Square in London is the City of Oslo's traditional Christmas gift to the City of Westminster.

The first tree was brought over in 1947 as a token of Norwegian appreciation of British friendship during the Second World War. When Norway was invaded by German forces in 1940, King Haakon VII escaped to Britain and a Norwegian government in exile was set up in London. To most Norwegians, London came to represent the spirit of freedom during those difficult years. From London, the latest war news was broadcast in Norwegian, along with a message and information network which became vital to the resistance movement and which gave the people in Norway inspiration and hope of liberation.

The tree has become a symbol of the close and warm relationship between the peoples of Britain and Norway. Norwegians are happy and proud that this token of friendship 'probably the most famous Christmas tree in the world' seems to have become so much a part of Christmas for Londoners.

The tree itself, a Norwegian spruce, is chosen with great care. Selected from one of the forests surrounding Oslo, it is earmarked for its place of honour in London several months, even years, in advance. The tree is usually 20–25 m (70ft) in height and anything between 50 and 60 years old. The Norwegian foresters who tend it with loving care describe it as 'the queen of the forest'

Crowds gather in central London for the 'switching on the lights' ceremony in December 1998.

where a spot has been allocated year after year to the Norwegian Christmas tree.

It takes several hours to put the tree up. Scaffolding is erected, the tree is winched up, and the base of its trunk pushed into soil and sand beneath the grey stone slabs. A dozen or more wooden wedges are driven in to make it secure. There is no other form of support. The tree stands there again as it did in the forest.

This is no ordinary Christmas tree. There cannot be many Christmas trees that have to be positioned in such a way that they will stand up to the prevailing southwesterly winds. One year, the wind took off three metres (4 ft) of the tip of the tree. That was just bad luck and could not be helped. But when, on another occasion, the tree snapped neatly in half as it was being unloaded from the ship, the people of Oslo came to the rescue and produced a replacement tree.

The ceremony of switching on the lights usually takes place on the first Thursday in December. There is a band, and trumpeters are playing. A choir sings Christmas carols as the Lord Mayor of Westminster arrives with his party. The floodlighting of the nearby National Gallery is especially dimmed for the occasion. The Christmas tree comes alive at the flick of a switch, into a sparkling, twinkling mass of lights. In line with Norwegian traditions, the lights are all white, the electrical bulbs being the twentieth-century equivalent of candlelight.

It is cut down one day in November. Most years, the first snow will have just fallen to brighten the otherwise dark forest. The cutting down ceremony is quite a grand occasion, with the mayor of Oslo and the British Ambassador to Norway usually present. The tree is then carried across the North sea by a Fred Olsen cargo ship sailing from Oslo to Felixstowe. It takes six or more men to handle the tree. They are specially contracted to haul it from the docks to Trafalgar Square

A crib provided by the Vicar of St Martins-in-the-Fields is erected on the west side of the square. It is dedicated at a special service on the Sunday after the lighting-up ceremony. The passing public may stop on their way home from work and join the carol singers every night until Christmas. During the carol singing, donations to selected charities are collected by volunteers.

to symbolise the sun and its warmth. In France, it is important that the Yule log comes from a fruit tree. In Yugoslavia the bringing in of the Yule log is still enacted in country districts, when men take to the forests in decorated carts to fetch the village's logs. A log is given to the head of each household, who scatters handfuls of grain, sweets and nuts over the cart as a gesture of prosperity and fertility. These small logs are cut off the main log, one for each of the Holy Family, and sometimes one for each member of the family. Any parts of the logs not burnt are kept until the New Year, when they are re-lit. The ashes are

Studding an orange with fresh cloves and hanging in on the tree with ribbon makes an unusual and pleasantly scented decoration.

eventually scattered on the land – an ancient survival of fertility rites.

In Latvia special magical meaning was attached to Christmas activities. One of these was dragging and rolling a log from neighbour to neighbour with a lot of frolicking, shouting and jumping over it. The log represented the past year's misfortunes, and when a significant and satisfactory amount of abuse had been done to the log, it was set on fire and burned.

In Slovenia the family gathered round the Yule log to pray, sing carols and have fun. It was used for fortune-telling. Girls poked at the smouldering stump to help it burn as quickly as possible. If it burned out before midnight, there would be a wedding in the house in the near future. In other places, they believed that the charcoal from the Christmas log had a special healing power, especially for illnesses of the throat. All these are remnants of pre-Christian beliefs and rituals when people tried to help the weakened sun in the period of the winter solstice. The fires also helped the spirits of the ancestors or the deceased to warm themselves.

Make your own Christmas Tree Decoration

Norwegian children make these attractive baskets to hang on the tree. They are strong enough to be filled with sweets. The baskets are very simple, but require nimble fingers.

All you need are sheets of coloured paper in two contrasting colours, a pair of sharp scissors and a small quantity of glue or paste.

1 Cut a strip of paper about 2cm/¾in wide and 15cm/6in long for the handle. Fold 2 sheets of paper about 20cm/8in square in half and from each one cut an extended  semi-circular shape, as shown. Make two parallel cuts, beginning at the base of each semi-circle and extending two-thirds of the way up. You now have two identical pieces of folded paper whose folded ends are cut into three long strips.

2 This is the tricky bit. Weave the legs through each other, always going through the centre of the strips in an alternating pattern. When the basket is complete it will open out as shown below.

3 Attach the handle to each side of the basket with a dab of glue.

A CHRISTMAS PROJECT

A Festive Wreath

This elegant decoration is surprisingly easy to make and very adaptable — you can vary the 'ingredients' to make it as simple or complicated as you like. If you don't want to hang the wreath on your door, use it as a table centrepiece instead.

A 28mm/11in diameter circle of florists' foam (Oasis)
Enough dried cones, nuts, seedheads etc to cover it generously — we used
    pine cones, walnuts, brazil nuts, small lotus heads, poppy seedheads, bunches of cinnamon sticks tied with raffia, dried morel mushrooms and dried aubergines
A can of gold spray paint
1m/3ft broad gold ribbon

1 Spray all the 'ingredients' with the gold paint. They

don't have to be completely covered in gold — you may prefer to have a mixture of gold and 'natural' colouring. Then spray the foam base — this will prevent the green showing through if you leave any gaps.

2 Press the stem of your first ingredient firmly into the base, then add another very close to it. Continue, mixing the ingredients to create a pattern

that pleases you, until the base is entirely covered. You will find that even nuts hold perfectly well if you press them in pointed side down, but you may prefer to glue them in place if you intend to hang the wreath up.

3 Tie the ribbon into a loose bow and attach it with a pin.

A CHRISTMAS PROJECT

A Christmas Mobile

As a change from wreaths, try making this attractive mobile from Poland.

3 x 25cm/10in piece of thin dowel
Thin florists' wire
Silver bead thread (available from craft shops or the haberdashery department of department stores) or strong cotton thread
About 40 beads in a variety of colours and sizes

1 Attach florists' wire to one end of each piece of dowel, leaving at least 7.5cm/3in of wire free each time.

2 Wrap a piece of plain coloured paper round each piece of dowel and glue into place.

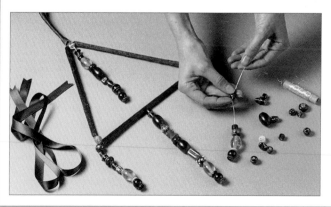

3 Thread a bead on to each piece of wire and twist the wires together so that the pieces of dowel form a triangle with a bead at each corner. Thread an assortment of beads on to 4 pieces of bead thread, 2 about 15cm/6in and 2 about 10cm/4in long, and secure each end. Attach the 2 shorter strings to the bottom corners of the triangle, and the 2 longer ones to the centre of the base and the apex of the triangle. Attach a loop of florists' wire to the top of the triangle and cover it with ribbon. Tie matching bows to the top and centre of the bottom of the triangle. Use the loop of wire to hang the mobile from a hook in the ceiling.

TU SCENDI DALLE STELLE

Testo e musica di **S. ALFONSO M. DE' LIGUORI**

Tempo di Barcarola

Tu scen—di dal—le

O COME, O COME, EMMANUEL

1. O come, O come, Em

Is-

In a Manger
W Żłobie Leży
Quartet

O du fröhliche, o du selige

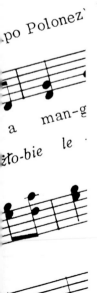

po Polonez'

a man-g

żło-bie le

le - sus,   to
Chry-stu-so-

Carols in Lincolnshire

This memory was contributed by Ann Goddard

One of the Christmas landmarks of my childhood was the choir carol singing. My father, rector of a country parish in rural Lincolnshire, would optimistically issue the call to arms during choir practice and in due course we would assemble a motley crew of singers selected not for mellifluence of voice but for willingness to turn out in the cold night air. The expedition was always a day or two before Christmas, and as I remember always cold and frosty with a million stars assisting our paraffin lanterns.

My dear old Pa led his choice in a resolute and nasal baritone, breaking into both the bass and tenor parts and followed doggedly by old Ned and the gentlemen of the choir. Ladies and children did their best with the soprano and alto parts, meekly echoing Julie, our leader, a mature lady of Wagnerian build and a voice to match for volume, but inclined to wander off key. We would number a dozen or so as we set off through the frosty darkness clutching our dog-eared carol sheets – unnecessary, as we all knew the old standards by heart.

The route through the village took in the principal farmers' houses, several stations along the main village street and the pub. We didn't sound too bad, in fact quite cheerful and seasonal accompanied by old Ned on his accordion. At each house we would be welcomed and given mince pies and half crowns after we had rendered ''ark the 'erald' or 'While Shepherds Watched' or 'Good King Wenceslas', dreaded by my sister Kate as she always had to sing the page's part. All my sisters and brother were automatically drafted into the choir and even today know most of *Hymns Ancient & Modern* by heart.

Our last call was always on the Squire in his large house, the front door strangely and exotically garlanded with a beribboned holly wreath. As we struck up 'Silent Night' the door would open, revealing the Squire and his family in evening dress, incredibly glamorous to our unsophisticated eyes. The Squire was always resplendent in a plum-coloured velvet jacket. My father would wish them all a Happy Christmas and ask for a request – it was invariably 'God Rest you Merry Gentlemen', an appropriate choice in view of the party's evidently enthusiastic celebration of Yuletide. Then in a magnificent yet casual way before our awestruck gaze the Squire would place a whole five-pound note in the collecting box.

Our carolling ended, we would all trudge back to the rectory to count our takings for the Church fund and celebrate with fruit cake, or mince pies and VP sherry. The angelic choir may have chimed with the music of the spheres, but their song was not more hearty and sincere than ours.

"O sanc
n Herder
ied" nach D

Christmas Music

All Christian nations have their own carols and everyone has their own favourites. Mark Elder, the conductor of worldwide experience, chooses 'O Come, O Come, Emmanuel'.

The word 'carol' originally meant a circling dance and has been associated with St Francis of Assisi and his installation of a crib in church during the Christmas season and singing or sometimes dancing round it. In Scotland, carol singers went on their rounds with brooms on their shoulders and as each door opened to them they would 'sweep in' luck.

In Malta the Christmas festival in the past was characterised more than any other by the music of bagpipes. Folk memory from the island of Gozo records that for the midnight service on Christmas Eve, bagpipes were played in the principal churches. During the Novena preceding Christmas, they performed up and down the streets and the drone of the bagpipes could be heard for miles around. The instrument was extremely crude and consisted of a mouthpiece attached to a calf's or dog's skin, and when inflated looked horribly like the living animal!

On Christmas Eve on the Isle of Man the *Oieíl Voirrey* service, the Eve of the Feast of Mary, is still held in some rural churches. The church is decorated with festoons of ivy and large branches of holly together with laurel and winter flowers, and the congregation arrives carrying specially made tallow candles decorated with ribbons. After a short service the clergyman leaves and the *Oieíl Voirrey* begins in earnest with the singing of carvals (Manx carols) until late into the night, if not the early hours of the morning. In the past some of these were new compositions written in the months leading up to Christmas. The carvals were written and sung in Manx Gaelic and now provide one of the most important collections of Manx literature.

Although written and sung at Christmas, most of the carvals are not about Christmas or the nativity but rather are songs about less seasonal themes such as sin and repentance, a particularly notorious one being the carval about evil women!

One of the most fascinating and enduring Welsh Christmas customs is *Y Plygain*, an early-morning carol service which once began at 3 a.m. The word comes from the Latin *pulli cantio* meaning cock-crow. Special coloured candles were prepared for the ceremony and people would often walk to the service in a candle-lit procession. The whole packed church would be ablaze with lighted candles and resound to the poetic Welsh carols specially written for the ceremony. As many as thirteen of these treasured carols were often sung before hunger drove the congregation homeward for a meal of cakes and strong ale. The *plygain* still persists in parts of mid-Wales but at the more civilised hour of 6 a.m.

A delightful custom which often followed the carols was the practice of bringing the plough indoors and depositing it under a table in the kitchen. The farm workers would then regale themselves with beer which was kept warm in small brass pans in every farmhouse They never forgot to pay tribute to the plough by anointing it with beer.

The pealing of bells on Christmas Eve in Spain calls families to *La Misa Del Gallo* (The Mass of the Rooster). The most beautiful of these services is held at the Monastery of Montserrat, high in the mountains near Barcelona. The highlight is a boys' choir performing the Mass in 'one pure voice'.

In Poland a popular form of carol singing was for three boys to travel around the villages carrying their *Szopka* – a miniature puppet theatre. Two of the boys would stand either side supporting the model theatre, while the third boy hid behind it and worked the tiny puppets. The two boys played a complicated part as they sang carols during the performance and managed in turn to accompany each other on the harmonica! The portable crib-theatre always portrayed the birth of the Infant Jesus, and the main villain was Herod.

For many Poles living away from their homeland, carols have continued to be a moving symbol of their national identity. Settled in Paris, Frédéric Chopin expressed his great yearning for Poland by entwining the sweet lullaby melody of the carol 'Sleep, Jesus, Sleep' into his Scherzo in G Flat Minor.

In Switzerland on the Sunday before Christmas star-singers (carollers) march through the streets, usually preceded by a star-bearer surrounded by white-clad angels. They are followed by Mary and Joseph with the donkey, shepherds and Three Wise Men. In public squares the group stops and plays scenes from the Christmas story. After a song in which the spectators join, they move on. Probably the most famous star-singers are those of Lucerne, Wettingen and Rapperswil. The carolling at Rapperswil is especially attractive because this is the winter quarters of the Knie Swiss National Circus. The King of the Moors sits on a real camel. Elegant Lipizzaner horses bear the other two kings to the main square in front of the church and the castle, where the carolling takes place. The shepherds come in with sheep which are rowed in a boat from the Canton of Schwyz across the lake. The great open-air staircase leading up to the castle is where the heavenly host take their places.

At Kerns in the Canton of Obwalden the procession of the three kings with their retinues starts in the church, from where they are solemnly sent forth. Good luck and God's blessing are wished to every family, and the three initials C, M, B (Caspar, Melchior and Balthasar) are written in consecrated chalk above the doors of the houses and stables. This is supposed to ward off the evil powers. All the while a troop of boys sing Christmas carols in front of the house.

SPECIAL TRADITIONS

Street Music in Italy

Margaret Hammond, an artist living in Rome who has been a friend of the author's for 80 years, writes:

'Here in the teeming noisy streets of Rome there is little to remind us of the countryside at Christmas time – but there is just one thing – a little sweet reedy sound that grows as it draws nearer to the house. It is a shepherd piper come down into the city from the mountains. He wears a sheepskin and his legs are wrapped round with bands of colour to keep his leggings tight. He plays a kind of bagpipe, something like the Scottish one, but much smaller. The music is very gentle and appealing and one cannot let him go by without throwing some coins from the window. He picks them up eagerly and goes on his way playing all the time.'

Many countries have a deep-rooted tradition of Christmas music, and carols play an important part in the celebrations, whether in church, in the home or in the village square. Original Dutch carols, however, are few and far between, which is why we have chosen to feature the one reproduced overleaf, set to an old Dutch melody.

Silent Night

According to *The Oxford Christmas Book for Children* by Roderick Hunt, the words of the beautiful carol 'Silent Night' were written in 1818 by Father Joseph Mohr, assistant pastor of the church of St Nicholas in the small town of Oberndorf in the Austrian Tyrol.

Late one afternoon, just before Christmas, Joseph Mohr was called out to bless a new-born baby. As he walked home through the snow, Father Mohr was deeply impressed by the beauty of the starlit night. He thought of the tiny baby he had just visited and wondered if was it on a night of such peace and stillness that the Holy Babe was born. When he reached home he put his feelings into words and wrote a poem.

The day before Christmas Eve it was discovered that mice had eaten the organ bellows and put the church organ out of action. The organ builder lived in Zillertal and could not get through the snow in time to repair the damage. What could be done about the music for the Christmas service? Father Mohr thought of his poem and showed it to his friend Franz Gruber, the church choirmaster. Franz took the poem home and, within an hour, had written a simple tune.

Franz Gruber's original manuscript for 'Stille Nacht' (top); **an Advent ceremony outside the 'Silent Night Church'** (left); **and the monument to Gruber and Father Joseph Mohr inside the church** (right).

church at Zillertal. Soon the beautiful carol was a favourite among the churchgoers of Zillertal who called it 'The Song of Heaven'.

Gradually the song made its way to Leipzig where it was heard by the city's Director of Music, who included it in a concert played before the Queen of Saxony. The Queen requested that it should be played in the palace on Christmas Eve 1832 so that her children could learn it.

In 1840 'Silent Night' was published in Leipzig under the title 'A Tyrolean Christmas Carol'. Its popularity began to spread through Europe, but still no one knew who had written the words and music. It was published again as a four-part song with 'author and composer unknown'. Some people believed it had been written by Michael and Joseph Haydn.

In 1854 the King of Prussia, Frederick Wilhelm IV, heard the song performed by the entire choir of the Imperial Church in Berlin. Immediately he declared that the song was to be sung at all Christmas concerts in his country that Christmas. He ordered his musicians to find out who had composed such beautiful music.

Everyone was delighted with it. That Christmas Eve, it was sung by Franz, Joseph and two women singers, with Joseph accompanying on his guitar.

When the organ builder came to repair the organ, Franz Gruber played the song. The organ builder was enchanted with it and asked if he could write down the words and music and play the song at his

Some time after this Franz Gruber's son heard about the song and recognised it as his father's music. After thirty-six years the carol that was loved by millions of people came back to the two men who had written it.

Jesus Tiny Baby

English words by Josepha Contoski/Music arranged by Edmund Contoski

Je - zus ma - lu   sień- ki   Le - ży   wsród sta -   jen - ki

I   drży z żim- na,   wzdy-cha nad Nim to ser - ce Ma -   teń - ki.

Jesus, Blessèd wonder,
Lay in lowly manger
With cold trembling,
While beside Him
Mother's heart was aching.

Mary was resourceful,
Covered Him with head shawl:
Then with fresh hay
Wrapped him gently,
Kept him warm on this day.
Jesus had no cradle
Nor a downy pillow
So in a small crib
Mary placed him
On hay, soft and mellow.

Little, Little Jesus

Old Dutch melody/Words by M. E. v. Ebbenhorst Tengbergen

Little, little Jesus, You are so cold.
Come and live in my heart.
And make Yourself a chimney.
We shall light a fire.
We shall cook porridge;
And bring your sweet Mother
Then we will all be content.

Penelope Wrong, a friend and neighbour of the author, contributes this wartime memory:

I have a most vivid childhood recollection of Christmas in Much Hadham. I would guess the year was 1944 and I would have been 10 years old. Wynches (the home of this book's compiler) was at that time a German prisoner of war camp.

Through a child's eyes these prisoners all seemed very old or very young – hardly older than myself. Our rector at that time was Revd Bernard Tower, and, in spite of the fact that he and his wife had lost a son and a son-in-law during the conflict, he exercised a remarkable ministry of reconciliation. In defiance of anti-fraternisation regulations he invited the German POWs to come to worship at St Andrew's Church every other week and some 50 or 60 used to come.

For the Christmas Eve carol service the regular parishioners sat in the south aisles and our German neighbours in the north aisle seats (I suppose one had to respect anti-fraternisation rules to that extent). The Germans sang superbly – perhaps they had a camp choir? My particular memory is of the simultaneous singing of 'Silent Night'/'Stille Nachte', each side of the church in their own tongue. I looked across the aisle during this carol to watch where this wonderful music was coming from, and was stunned to see these young men singing their hearts out while tears coursed down their cheeks – they must have been so homesick. I have never forgotten that night.

Lighting candles in St Cosmas and Damian church, Moscow.

Cribs

A representation of the Nativity scene is a common feature of Christmas decorations across Europe, especially in Catholic countries. Here, the crib is a focus for the celebration, with the tree (if there is one) placed somewhere less important. (By contrast, in Orthodox countries cribs are less significant and the tree is the focal point of the decorations.) In Sicily families create *un presepio* to encourage the spiritual atmosphere, so that presents and other commercial considerations do not predominate. In Cracow every year, a competition is held for the most beautiful handmade crib. These creations are displayed in the market square. Nativity scenes arranged in churches also have a long-standing tradition. The mechanical crèche in the Capuchin church in Warsaw continually receives new items. Next to the donkey, ox and camels on which the Magi travelled, one can also notice a train, a bus or even an aeroplane!

Cribs are usually very beautiful — even homemade ones may be the work of gifted amateurs. In Austria the *Krippen* are

A 20th-century Dutch crib by Gerard Hérnan, from the Houtzager Collection.

The traditional crib doesn't need to use traditional materials. This Christmas group, from Corsica, is made from slate and gravel. The raw materials have not been processed, simply glued together.

often family heirlooms. In other countries using natural materials adds to the mystique of the crib. Composing such displays — the *Pessebres* — is still a Christmas tradition in Andorra. Young parents start with a few pieces and add to them year by year. The use of natural materials is considered important and the gathering of moss, grass, twigs and stones is still an occasion for a family outing to the lower valleys.

The origin of the crib

The first crib was made in the village of Greccio in Italy on Christmas night, 1223. A procession of shepherds, peasants, carpenters and simple people set out for the Grotto which Giovani di Greccio had prepared for St Francis with the approval of Pope Honorius III.

An early 19th-century 'countryside' crib from Slovenia.

A detail from the 18th-century Neapolitan crib from the Houtzager collection in Holland.

This homemade crib from France (above) could almost be based on *The Adoration of the Magi* by **Carlo Dolci** (below), **painted in the seventeenth century. In both groups Mary and the Baby Jesus sit in the centre surrounded by worshippers; the modern version even echoes the rays of light shining down from heaven.**

One of the earliest three-dimensional representations of Christ's birth was made by the Tuscan sculptor, Arnolfo di Cambio in 1282 in the chapel of the Holy Crèche in Rome. The chapel was the repository of what was believed to be a relic of the very manger in which Christ had been laid as a new-born babe.

The Christmas Crib Collection

Holland possesses one of the largest and most representative Christmas crib collections in the world. It took Mrs Elisabeth Houtzager fifty years to amass her collection of 800 'groups' from all over the world, including figures from Russia, the Caucasus, Mexico, India and Upper Volta.

One of the largest items in her collection is an 18th century Neapolitan crib which has small earthenware figures, painted in many colours, which have been gradually added to over the years. The figures are extremely delicate and beautifully modelled. The scene shows a ruined Roman temple, the roof of which supports the Holy Family surrounded by the shepherds. One is playing the bagpipes, while another plays the flute. Above float the angels and the Star of Bethlehem. To the right the Three Kings come riding under a bridge. Beyond them is an inn and houses surrounding the market-place. In front of the inn several people are eating spaghetti, while the landlord brings a bottle of wine and a woman entertains them with an accordion. The cook can be seen at work inside, while a slaughtered sheep, a goose, and large hams are displayed outside. Upstairs, a woman is doing her washing with a scrubbing board on the balcony where

fruits and vegetables are hung up to dry. Every aspect of everyday life is shown: the shoemaker, the blacksmith at his anvil, traders selling fruit, vegetables, fish, cheese and sausages, while the farmer tends the farm animals. The whole scene is charming, and beautifully composed.

Living Cribs

The most interesting cribs are the so-called 'living crèches' arranged on Christmas Eve in natural surroundings with live actors, sheep and other livestock. Something special is the now traditional living crèche in Postojna Cave, Slovenia, one of the world's largest karst caves, where the figures of the event in Bethlehem are arrayed among the marvellous world of stalactites and stalagmites. This spectacle, of course, has a primarily tourist character.

In Italy too, one of the most popular entertainments during the Christmas season is to visit the *Presepi*. These are elaborate Christmas cribs, so large that they have to be housed in a separate room, even in the churches. In Rome it is quite usual to give up half a day to do a tour of the most famous of these *Presepi*. They are advertised outside the churches in large letters with rather vulgar electric signs, such as a flashing comet with a long tail and arrows pointing to a side door where one may queue to enter.

In Hungary, especially in the villages of Transylvania, there used to be a tradition for small groups of children to go round to neighbouring houses carrying a crib in the form of a model church. They would be dressed as Joseph, shepherds or even King Herod. Someone would recite a recognised verse asking for hospitality, and, upon being made welcome, they would enter the home and sing carols round the crib. Another custom was 'Looking for Lodgings'. A small group carried a picture of the Holy Family to some of the more prosperous houses, asking for lodgings. Any gifts received would be distributed among the poorer dwellings.

SPECIAL TRADITIONS

The Living Crib in Malta

In Malta children enthusiastically help their parents to create the crib from papier mâché, and little figures of Mary, Joseph and Baby Jesus as well as diverse village people and farm animals portraying the nativity scene. Indeed some people take this so seriously that they set aside entire rooms in their homes for large cribs depicting the nativity and surrounding scenery. These are then open to the public. Visitors are encouraged to donate a small contribution thus raising much needed funds for charitable causes. Annual competitions are held for the best presented presepju (crib) on the island. Whether in church or at home, cribs in Malta are decorated with masses of pots of watercress. The seeds are sown in a shallow layer of cotton wool in late November or early December, watered regularly and kept in the dark to enable the watercress to grow luxuriantly long and milky white. The result is a magnificent display of 'angel hair' watercress placed at the side and in front of cribs. In church, the altar is decorated also with potted poinsettias, a plant native to the island.

Fireworks and festive lighting in Rotunda Square, Mosta, in Malta.

Celebrations and Customs

In the St Pholien area of Liège, Belgium, at 10 p.m. on Christmas Eve begins the *Marche à l'Etoile* – a candle-lit procession led by someone carrying a large star, followed by worshippers including farmers with donkeys, cows, sheep and goats. Their destination is the Place St Pholien where a crib is set up and costumed characters mingle with the crowd. There is free distribution of hot wine, boudin and *bouquètes* – pancakes made with buckwheat and sprinkled with sultanas or sugar.

As part of the preparations for Christmas, village girls in many parts of Slovenia used to carry a statue of the Virgin with special ceremony for nine consecutive evenings, each evening into a different house. Today, this custom is followed only among the Slovene minority community in Friuli-Venezia Giulia, Italy, who call it 'The Nine of Christmas'.

In Seville in southern Spain on December 8th each year, ten elaborately costumed boys celebrate the Feast of the Immaculate Conception in front of the cathedral. The ritual dance, known as *Los Seises* (The Dance of Six), consists of a series of movements and gestures that are said to be emotionally moving and beautiful.

On Christmas Eve in Malta it has long been a tradition for young children to walk in procession behind a life-size statue of Baby Jesus as it is carried around the streets in towns and villages. This is accompanied by the singing of Christmas carols in Maltese, English or Italian. A very popular Maltese carol is *Ninni, ta tibkix izjed* (Go to sleep and cry no more). Processions are usually organised by local religious societies which undertake to prepare children for their First Holy Communion.

An old custom in Holland on Three Kings Day (January 6th) used to be Star Singing. A man would walk the streets of the town with a revolving star on a stick and he sang his songs to anyone who would listen! This has now become a children's festivity, mostly in the south of the country. Children dress up like kings and with their star and lantern visit houses, three at

A Croatian Christmas procession by Ivan Lackovic Croata.

SPECIAL TRADITIONS

Wassailing

The traditional song used on Christmas Eve served as a link between the jollities connected with Christmas and those which are connected with agricultural festivals. Wassailing was originally a tree ceremony, to ensure that trees were fruitful in the coming season.

Wassail, wassail
All round the town
Your cup is so white
And your beer is so brown

Chorus :
For its our wassail
And a jolly wassail
And joy be to you
For it's our wassail

Missus and master
Now we are come here
Give us a cup
Of your best Christmas beer

In Wales wassailing often meant carrying an ornate twelve-handled wassail bowl from house to house where wassailers would sing verses to be answered by those within. In the wassail bowl were cakes and apples covered by warm beer infused with rich spices from India. They would sing at the door to gain entry whereupon they would enjoy the contents of the bowl before departing with it replenished. On their departure they would sing a verse of blessing to their hosts:

Hir einioes a hir dyddiau a hir flynddau hardd
A gaffoch i fywín frwythlon fel hir blanhigion gardd,
Gael gweled plant ac wyrion yn llawnion yn un llu

(Long life, long days and long beautiful years may you have; to live a fruitful life like pure garden plants, to see many children and grandchildren flourish).

Wassail the trees, that they may bear
You many a plum and many a pear:
For more or less fruits they will bring,
As you do give them wassailing.
Robert Herrick

a time. Having sung their song they are rewarded with sweets, small change or fruit.

In Romania Christmas Day is known as 'Second Day'. There is a custom on Second Day of wandering from house to house singing Christmas songs, or for groups of people, wearing animal masks and dressed in animal skins, to travel up and down the village roads, singing and blowing trumpets, accompanied by the beating of drums.

An English custom, practised in Wiltshire, was the 'Christmas bull'. The head of the bull, with great bottle eyes, large horns and lolling tongue, was manipulated by a man stooping inside a body composed of a broomstick, a hide of sacking and a rope tail. The bull knocked on the door with its horns, and if allowed to enter chased the young people round the house with fearsome curvettings and bellowings.

Oxford covered market has a boar's head competition every Christmas. The butchers decorate the heads with artistry and ingenuity and they are positioned on 'a sea of lard, white and glistening'. Children on their way home are keen, unofficial judges.

There is also an old carol, known as the Boar's Head Carol, which is sung in Christ Church at Christmas. Oxford's preoccupation with the boar is because the last wild boar killed in England was in the area, hence the naming of Boar's Hill.

The Boar's Head in hand bear I
Bedeck'd with bays and rosemary;
And I pray on, my masters, be merry.

In Estonia mummers dressed up as animals and one person played the part of Goose, generally teasing and vexing everyone, especially the children, and making people pay forfeits to escape his clutches! Another popular Yuletide mummer was the 'He-goat'. He had a switch tied to his backside which he dipped into water, then chased and

Maltese adults and children join together in the traditional street procession.

On Innocents' Day (December 28th), *tepeûkanje* is still a custom in Slovenia. Children go from house to house, hitting the adults on the buttocks with switches and receiving presents. This custom has its basis in the biblical story of Herod's slaughter of boys under the age of two in Bethlehem and its surroundings. However, this is just the Christian version of an older custom that reaches into the pre-Christian period and its concept of the procession of children's souls. The beating with a switch was intended to help save the adults from the dark troublesome spirits of the ancestors that would therefore not harm them in their lives.

In Macedonia there have been many customs and beliefs connected with the ritual fires lit to celebrate Christmas Eve. These fires must not be confused with the lighting and burning of the traditional log. During the first night members of the family do not sleep but remain awake to keep a vigil, consequently the night is known as the 'Awake Night'. In the region of Debar, believers took care that a piece of unburned wood would remain, which was lighted and extinguished with

wine every night from Christmas to Epiphany – this was to ensure the preservation of the cattle! The importance of fire – the bigger the better – concerned man's aim to imitate the great source of energy from the sky. Primitive man believed that strong fires burning on earth could help the weak, barely visible winter sun.

In the Twente region of north-east Holland, the old tradition of blowing the midwinter horn is being revived. The horn – 1.2 metres long – is made from wood. In some of the Catholic churches the 'blowers' play this instrument at the Christmas Eve midnight service. On Boxing Day the veterans play for a wager and the sound of this strange, penetrating tone can be heard any time from the first Sunday in Advent to January 6th.

According to folklore beliefs in Macedonia, Greece and Bulgaria, during the twelve days between Christmas and Epiphany when Jesus was not baptised, various evil demons, witches, vampires etc. perform their deeds and try to hurt men. On the day of baptism, all their actions are paralysed!

In Bulgaria these are the so-called 'Dirty Days' when Earth and Sky were believed to be unchristened and when evil spirits of all kinds were particularly active! They were thought to inhabit caves, waterfalls, places where ivy grew, ravines and other desolate and sinister places such as deserted water-mills, where they slept for most of the year, but from sunset to cock-crow, during the 'Dirty Days', they would run wild and attack people! In the popular imagination, the *Karakondzho* took both animal and human form – a hairy man with horns and a tail, or a horse with wings and a human head. It was thought that they pounced on unsuspecting people and rode – or lured them – over cliffs or into deep water. The obvious thing was not to go out at night, but if obliged to, to carry a piece of iron, some garlic or an onion which had lain on the Christmas Eve feast table.

In Norway in the past, barn doors would be marked with a cross to keep away evil spirits – the cross was also used as a

SPECIAL TRADITIONS

Keeping the Goblins Away

In almost every Greek home, the main symbol of the season is a shallow wooden bowl suspended by a piece of wire around the rim; from that hangs a sprig of basil which is wrapped around a wooden cross. A small amount of water is kept in the bowl to keep the basil alive and fresh. There is a special ritual which is connected with the basil and the cross. Once a day, a family member dips the basil and cross into some holy water and uses it to sprinkle the water in each room of the house. This ritual is believed to keep the Killintzaroi away from the house. There are a number of beliefs connected with the Killintzaroi which are a species of goblins or sprites, who only appear during the twelve-day period from Christmas to Epiphany (January 6th). These creatures are believed to emerge from the centre of the earth and to slip into people's houses down the chimney. More mischievous than actually evil, the Killintzaroi do teasing tricks like extinguishing fires, riding astride people's backs, braiding the horses tails, and turning the milk sour. To further repel these sprites, the hearth is kept burning day and night throughout the twelve days.

SPECIAL TRADITIONS

Mummers

In Russia by the third day of Christmas, the young became restless for further excitement or entertainment, and in War and Peace, there is a lively, colourful account of the Christmas tradition of mummery, packing themselves into sleighs in order to visit and disturb good friends and neighbours who might be sleepily recovering from the over-indulgences of the Christmas table!

'The mummers (some of the house-serfs dressed up as bears, Turks, tavern-keepers and fine ladies – awe-inspiring or comic figures) at first huddled bashfully together in the vestibule, bringing in with them the cold and hilarity from outside. Then, hiding behind one another, they pushed into the ballroom where, at first shyly but afterwards with ever-increasing merriment and zeal, they started singing, dancing and playing Christmas games.... Half an hour later there appeared among the mummers in the ballroom an old lady in a farthingale – this was Nikolai. A Turkish girl was Petya. Dimmler was a clown. A hussar was Natasha, and a Circassian youth Sonya with burnt

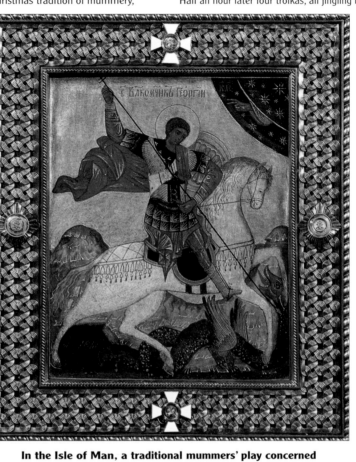

In the Isle of Man, a traditional mummers' play concerned St George killing a Turkish knight in battle, a much modified version of the familiar story of George and the Dragon. This 15th-century icon is of Russian origin, showing how widespread the legend of St George is.

cork moustaches and eyebrows... The young people decided their costumes were so good they ought to be displayed somewhere else.... Half an hour later four troikas, all jingling bells, drove up to the porch, their runners crunching and creaking over the frozen snow...

Pelageya Danilovna Melyukov was sitting in the drawing-room surrounded by her daughters whom she was doing her best to keep amused... when the steps and voices of the visitors began to echo through from the hall. Hussars, fine ladies, witches, clowns and bears, clearing their throats in the vestibule and wiping the hoar-frost from their faces, came into the ballroom where candles were hurriedly lit. The clown – Dimmler – and the lady – Nikolai – opened the dance. Surrounded by shrieking children, the mummers hid their faces and, disguising their voices, bowed to their hostess... After Russian country-dances and choruses Madame Melyukov made the serfs and gentry form into one large circle; a ring, a string and a silver rouble were fetched and they all began playing games.

decoration on bread, as a pattern on butter, or on the ceiling over the Christmas table.

At Christmas and New Year, young Russian girls spent much time predicting their future, and midnight was the mystic hour.

A large mirror was put in the room, one or two candles were lighted and special words were repeated. The girls were seated in front of the mirror and desperately gazing into it – the man they saw first was considered to be their future husband!

SPECIAL TRADITIONS

Mummers

In Russia by the third day of Christmas, the young became restless for further excitement or entertainment, and in War and Peace, there is a lively, colourful account of the Christmas tradition of mummery, packing themselves into sleighs in order to visit and disturb good friends and neighbours who might be sleepily recovering from the over-indulgences of the Christmas table!

'The mummers (some of the house-serfs dressed up as bears, Turks, tavern-keepers and fine ladies – awe-inspiring or comic figures) at first huddled bashfully together in the vestibule, bringing in with them the cold and hilarity from outside. Then, hiding behind one another, they pushed into the ballroom where, at first shyly but afterwards with ever-increasing merriment and zeal, they started singing, dancing and playing Christmas games.... Half an hour later there appeared among the mummers in the ballroom an old lady in a farthingale – this was Nikolai. A Turkish girl was Petya. Dimmler was a clown. A hussar was Natasha, and a Circassian youth Sonya with burnt

cork moustaches and eyebrows... The young people decided their costumes were so good they ought to be displayed somewhere else.... Half an hour later four troikas, all jingling bells, drove up to the porch, their runners crunching and creaking over the frozen snow...

Pelageya Danilovna Melyukov was sitting in the drawing-room surrounded by her daughters whom she was doing her best to keep amused... when the steps and voices of the visitors began to echo through from the hall. Hussars, fine ladies, witches, clowns and bears, clearing their throats in the vestibule and wiping the hoar-frost from their faces, came into the ballroom where candles were hurriedly lit. The clown – Dimmler – and the lady – Nikolai – opened the dance. Surrounded by shrieking children, the mummers hid their faces and, disguising their voices, bowed to their hostess... After Russian country-dances and choruses Madame Melyukov made the serfs and gentry form into one large circle; a ring, a string and a silver rouble were fetched and they all began playing games.

In the Isle of Man, a traditional mummers' play concerned St George killing a Turkish knight in battle, a much modified version of the familiar story of George and the Dragon. This 15th-century icon is of Russian origin, showing how widespread the legend of St George is.

decoration on bread, as a pattern on butter, or on the ceiling over the Christmas table.

At Christmas and New Year, young Russian girls spent much time predicting their future, and midnight was the mystic hour.

A large mirror was put in the room, one or two candles were lighted and special words were repeated. The girls were seated in front of the mirror and desperately gazing into it – the man they saw first was considered to be their future husband!

Stockings and Presents

Not every country believes in hanging up stockings. In some European countries children put out their shoes for presents on December 5th, the Eve of St Nicholas Day, though nowadays a second lot of presents are sometimes put under the tree. In Holland, the children receive their gifts on December 6th but first they have to use ingenuity and imagination to solve the clues which lead to the 'hard to find parcels' which are not necessarily wrapped in decorative paper. Some people compose poems which are attached to the gifts. It is possible in a subtle way to leg-pull or even mention past incidents or remarks that went amiss – a unique moment to make the peace!

Many other countries decorate the tree on Christmas Eve and the room is then locked while the Christ Child brings the presents. These are usually opened after the celebratory Christmas Eve meal and the singing of carols around the tree.

Christmas presents in Sweden are known as Christmas 'knocks' – *julklapp*. On Christmas Eve people used to tiptoe up to a front door with a wrapped present, knock hard, and, as it was opened, throw the present inside – hopefully unbreakable! This all had to be done without being recognised, because often the Christmas knock would have a sarcastic or even malicious rhyming message on the wrapper.

A CHRISTMAS PROJECT

Making Your Own Christmas Stocking

Christmas stockings are really more like long, loose-fitting socks, and can be made very simply from two pieces of material cut into the appropriate shape and stitched together. For something a bit more elegant, try this.

2 Sew up the back seam of the lining material to form a shoe, and stuff it with cotton wadding so that it holds its shape.

4 Sew decorative beads or buttons on to the front of the boot and hem the top with lace.

1 Cut a template out of stiff card in the shape of a high-heeled boot. Use it to cut two shapes – one in lining material, of foot and heel only, and one in patterned material, of the whole boot.

3 Wrap the patterned material round the shoe, pull into a boot shape and stitch up the back seam.

5 As a finishing touch, sew a strip of piping around the ankle.

In Greece, January 1st, the Feast of St Basil, is the time for presents. In Spain, it is not Father Christmas or St Nicholas who brings presents, but the Three Wise Men. The children's favourite is Balthazar, who rides a donkey and is the one believed to leave gifts. To receive them, children fill their shoes with straw and leave them on a doorstep or windowsill on the eve of Epiphany, January 5th. The Three Kings are generous, but those who have behaved badly during the year may be left only a piece of coal.

Giving Christmas and New Year's presents has only been known in Slovenia for about 70 years. Rural Slovenia only knew present giving on Christmas Eve in the form of walnuts or hazelnuts, and even this was mainly symbolic.

Markets

Germany boasts the most spectacular Christmas markets in the world. The market in Munich is known as the Christ Child Market. It is said to date back for over 600 years and was mentioned as early as 1310. Almost the entire marketplace is covered with wooden stalls where all kinds of goods are set out for sale. Small children believe that the Christ Child buys the gifts there. Walking through such a market is a real experience. The smell of fir resin and roasted almonds – the little stoves where sausages are fried – the lights, and the songs and music fill the air – if snow falls, a hushed mood prevails. In the early dusk the atmosphere is a sensation between fairyland and a religious service.

'Operation Christmas Stocking': Christmas morning for Victorian children in the care of the NSPCC.

Although decorated fans were once very popular, it is rare for their subjects to be of a religious nature. This beautiful 19th-century example, portraying the Nativity, is in the private collection of Hélène Alexander at the Fan Museum in Greenwich, south London, not far from the Millennium Dome.

The Story of Hamleys

When William Hamley first opened a toy shop in London in 1760, Westminster Bridge had just opened to traffic – horses and carts. Even gas lights would not illuminate the city's streets for another half a century. But William Hamley, a Cornishman from Bodmin, was not put off. He filled his cramped Holborn shop with every toy he could find, rag dolls and tin solders, hoops and wooden horses, because he wanted the finest toy shop in the world. He even called it the 'Noah's Ark'.

A Silesian Christmas

Mrs E G Beaton writes of her childhood in Lower Silesia, now part of Poland:

Christmas Eve is the most important day. Christkindel (Christ Child) would deliver the presents. As soon as it got dark, we children would get very excited. The living-room door was closed all day long, because one could never see Christkindel – naturally Father Christmas would decorate the Christmas Tree, which was never put up before Christmas Eve. After a Christmas dinner of carp, smoked pork and sausages cooked in a special brown sauce, we would listen to see if we could hear anything that was going on in the living-room. Suddenly a bell would chime. That meant that Christkindel had finished putting presents under the tree and had flown out of the window to the other children. What a sight! Real candles were burning on the pine tree, decorated with silver tinsel and silver balls. Standing under the tree was something I longed for – a doll's cot! In the cot a baby doll was tucked under a blanket with a little feeding bottle next to it.'

War Christmas

Lady Holland-Martin shares this recollection of a wartime Christmas:

Up to the war our Christmases were always the same, and very conventional, with lots of family and presents. But with the war everything became more expensive and difficult to find. So we evolved a plan. We invited lots of friends and we all had to provide five presents not costing more than a pound in total, wrapped in newspaper. These were put in a large container. We each took five, swapping was encouraged and there were no hurt feelings. So if my father got a plastic car he could exchange it for a box of matches. Lots of the presents were home-made. Try it now. It was fun.

The first modern Christmas card

Cards and Wrapping

The Christmas card was a 19th-century British invention. It was a natural development from the earlier custom of exchanging seasonal letters or visiting cards, embellished with greetings, and also drew on the well-established tradition of sending valentine cards.

The history of printed cards of good wishes for the New Year goes back to the early years of European engraving and printing. A German engraving of 1466 shows Jesus as a little boy with a halo, stepping forward on a decorated flower. Behind is a wooden crucifix. *Ein guot sellig ior* (good and happy year) is engraved on a floating scroll. The wording on these early cards almost always gives New Year wishes, while the design is usually of the Infant Jesus. These are the forerunners of both Christmas and New Year cards. They were printed from woodblocks and coloured by hand.

The first modern card was designed in 1843 by John Calcott Horsley at the suggestion of Henry Cole. It shows a homely family party, framed in a rustic trellis with vines twining through it. The family are all raising their glasses in a toast, while the small children are eating plum pudding. Two side panels represent the spirit of Christmas charity: on one side the poor are fed, while on the other they are given warm clothing.

About 1,000 copies of this card were sold, at one shilling a time. Christmas cards soon caught on, and their use became widespread after the introduction in 1870 of the cheap postal rate for cards and unsealed envelopes. By the 1880s five million cards and letters were being sent at Christmas in Britain and the practice soon spread overseas.

Today, the use of Christmas cards is widespread, and millions are sent every year. In the trade, Christmas cards are classified into six types. 'Cute' cards and traditional cards are the most popular, though the liking for cute cards is very British and it is difficult to sell them abroad. The other categories are: religious, juvenile, humorous and graphic. Humorous cards were very popular in the 19th century, but cute cards are a new departure. Biblical themes have never been common, even in the 19th century when the bulk of the population went to church. The most recent development has been the sending of charity cards, where a proportion of the proceeds goes to a particular charity.

A CHRISTMAS PROJECT

Making Your Own Cards

A handmade Christmas card is a delight to receive and not at all difficult to do, provided you start early enough. Early in the year start collecting interesting papers and cards, pieces of ribbon and braid and gold decorations.

1 From a piece of card cut a rectangle 17 x 25cm (6¾ x 9¾in) and fold it in half. Cut a piece of contrasting crepe paper or tissue paper slightly smaller than the card and use it as lining – fix it inside the card with a very small amount of glue. Cut sheets of recycled coloured paper into pieces 10cm (4in) wide and slightly longer than the card. Cut along each length with pinking shears, then glue to the front of the cards, leaving an equal margin on each side.

2 Cut a simple shape – a tree, bell, star, angel etc – in varying colours from handmade or recycled paper in a contrasting or toning colour. Glue the shape to the front of the card.

3 Glue a bow made from metallic braid or gold cord on front.

4 Or slip a piece of coloured cord inside the card and tie it in a bow so that it sits firmly round the spine without crushing it.

A CHRISTMAS PROJECT

Making Simple Presents Special

As with homemade cards, the recipient of a gift of homemade mincemeat will be touched that you have gone to the trouble of making something that is readily available commercially. This is one of Mrs Beeton's recipes, dating from the middle of the 19th century. Using nothing more complicated that a square of pretty fabric and a matching ribbon makes this a delightfully personal present. Luxury shop-bought foods or cosmetics could be 'wrapped' in the same way.

Makes 2.5kg/5 lb • *Preparation time: 1 hour*

3 large lemons
3 large apples
450g/1lb seedless raisins
450g/1lb dried currants
450g/1lb shredded suet
1kg/2lb brown sugar
30g/1oz each shredded candied citron, candied orange
peel and fresh lemon peel (with pith removed)
250ml/8oz brandy
2 tablespoons orange marmalade

Grate the rinds of the lemons and squeeze out the juice. Strain it and boil the remainder of the lemons until tender enough to pulp or chop very finely.

Bake the apples in a preheated oven at 180°C/350°F/Gas Mark 4 for 30–45 minutes, until very soft. Remove the skin and core of the apples and add their pulp to the lemons.

Add the remaining ingredients one by one, mixing everything very thoroughly together.

Store in jars with closely fitting lids for a fortnight before using.

Crackers

Linking arms with our neighbours around the Christmas table to pull crackers, donning a paper hat and reading out bad jokes is to most people as integral a part of the celebrations as holly, mistletoe and plum pudding. But – unlike these traditions, which date back to pre-Christian times –the idea of putting a small gift and hat into a cardboard tube and then pulling it apart for fun was first thought of in the nineteenth century and became part of the Christmas festivities even more recently.

The cracker was invented by an enterprising Victorian named Tom Smith, who as a young boy in 1830 worked in a bakery in London. His employers were often commissioned to supply elaborate cakes for weddings, and Smith began creating new designs and decorations for these confections. He soon started his own business, selling cake decorations, sweets and party novelties such as flags and streamers. Much of his success can be attributed to his constant efforts to offer his customers new and exciting ideas for their parties

Crackers are meant to be fun – go for bright colours, metallic wrapping paper, multi-coloured ribbon and anything else you fancy to brighten them up. Snaps, mottoes and decorations are available from craft shops or shops specialising in parties.

Smith's search for inspiration frequently took him abroad. In Paris in 1840 he came across an idea for selling confectionery that was new to him: a sugared almond wrapped in a twist of tissue paper and called a bonbon. His fertile brain instantly saw that this had potential as another party novelty.

Although bonbons were very popular in Paris, they at first failed to impress Tom Smith's English market. After all, it was just unwrapping a sweet. But Smith was convinced that he had a winning idea — it was just a matter of making his bonbons more exciting. Legend has it that inspiration came one day when he was listening to the logs crackle and snap in his fireplace. What the bonbons needed was sound!

Within a year, Tom Smith was selling a much larger version of his bonbons, which he called 'Cosaques'. The wrapping now included an explosive snap, a motto and a gift. This was obviously just what the British public was waiting for: demand for Smith's 'crackers', as they were soon called, far exceeded what he was able to supply from his existing premises.

The business continued to expand and, after Tom Smith's death, his three sons carried on their father's work. One of these sons, Walter, is credited with the idea of including hats made out of tissue paper in the crackers.

Crackers reached the height of their popularity in the early years of the 20th century. At this time they were far more topical than they are today, with mottoes referring to current events and fashions, rather than the old jokes and bad puns to which we are used. Early Tom Smith catalogues also show a wide range of designs. Some were elaborate table decorations adorned with artificial flowers. There were Funniosities and Japanese Curiosities, rather alarming-sounding Animated Insects and Reptiles, and musical crackers containing motor horns, cat calls, bird warblers and bagpipes. Special events inspired the creation of special crackers — there was even a design in honour of the Suffragettes.

Wrapping presents in the form of crackers can transform them into something special. Slip the present inside the inner tube of a toilet roll or cylinder of thin card. Cut a piece of paper three times the length of the cylinder and wrap it around. Tie a ribbon at each end of the cylinder and frill out the ends to give a cracker effect.

Throughout this time, crackers had no particular association with Christmas — that emphasis emerged gradually as the 20th century progressed. The British Royal Family has always been a great patron of Tom Smith crackers and regularly orders them for its Christmas celebrations.

Nowadays much of the cracker-making process is automated (although the Tom Smith company still positions the 'snap' manually) and handmade crackers are a luxury. One manufacturer, inspired by the quality of crackers the founders remembered having as children, uses fabric rather than paper so that the crackers can be reused and supplies each one with four snaps, four mottoes and four hats, so that the same cracker can be pulled and enjoyed on Christmas Eve, Christmas Day, Boxing Day and New Year's Eve.

Smith's search for inspiration frequently took him abroad. In Paris in 1840 he came across an idea for selling confectionery that was new to him: a sugared almond wrapped in a twist of tissue paper and called a bonbon. His fertile brain instantly saw that this had potential as another party novelty.

Although bonbons were very popular in Paris, they at first failed to impress Tom Smith's English market. After all, it was just unwrapping a sweet. But Smith was convinced that he had a winning idea – it was just a matter of making his bonbons more exciting. Legend has it that inspiration came one day when he was listening to the logs crackle and snap in his fireplace. What the bonbons needed was sound!

Within a year, Tom Smith was selling a much larger version of his bonbons, which he called 'Cosaques'. The wrapping now included an explosive snap, a motto and a gift. This was obviously just what the British public was waiting for: demand for Smith's 'crackers', as they were soon called, far exceeded what he was able to supply from his existing premises.

The business continued to expand and, after Tom Smith's death, his three sons carried on their father's work. One of these sons, Walter, is credited with the idea of including hats made out of tissue paper in the crackers.

Crackers reached the height of their popularity in the early years of the 20th century. At this time they were far more topical than they are today, with mottoes referring to current events and fashions, rather than the old jokes and bad puns to which we are used. Early Tom Smith catalogues also show a wide range of designs. Some were elaborate table decorations adorned with artificial flowers. There were Funniosities and Japanese Curiosities, rather alarming-sounding Animated Insects and Reptiles, and musical crackers containing motor horns, cat calls, bird warblers and bagpipes. Special events inspired the creation of special crackers – there was even a design in honour of the Suffragettes.

Wrapping presents in the form of crackers can transform them into something special. Slip the present inside the inner tube of a toilet roll or cylinder of thin card. Cut a piece of paper three times the length of the cylinder and wrap it around. Tie a ribbon at each end of the cylinder and frill out the ends to give a cracker effect.

Throughout this time, crackers had no particular association with Christmas – that emphasis emerged gradually as the 20th century progressed. The British Royal Family has always been a great patron of Tom Smith crackers and regularly orders them for its Christmas celebrations.

Nowadays much of the cracker-making process is automated (although the Tom Smith company still positions the 'snap' manually) and handmade crackers are a luxury. One manufacturer, inspired by the quality of crackers the founders remembered having as children, uses fabric rather than paper so that the crackers can be reused and supplies each one with four snaps, four mottoes and four hats, so that the same cracker can be pulled and enjoyed on Christmas Eve, Christmas Day, Boxing Day and New Year's Eve.

A CHRISTMAS PROJECT

Making Your Own Crackers

A piece of piping 5cm/2in in diameter and about 40cm/16in long (from a builders' merchant or DIY store)

Stiff card

1 A4 sheet of the thinnest paper your stationer can sell you (properly called scrim), for the lining

A sheet of crepe paper 20cm/8in wide

2 30cm/12in pieces of curling ribbon

Sellotape

Snaps, paper hats, small presents and mottoes (from a craft shop)

1 Cut the stiff card into 3 pieces, one 5 x 9cm/2 x 3½in square for the centre and two 5 x 7.5 cm/2 x 3in for the ends. Find the centre of the pipe. Using a knife or strips of sticky tape, mark where the card will fit. Leave a gap of 4cm/1½in between each piece of card. Wrap the larger piece of card round the pipe and secure with Sellotape – not too tightly, as it must slide off. Wrap the smaller pieces of card round each end.

2 Sellotape the snap to the card lengthwise.

3 Wrap the lining paper around the pipe and fasten lightly with Sellotape, then wrap the crepe paper around that and fasten as before. Very gently slide the piping out from the centre of the cracker.

4 Squeeze one end of the cracker together at the gap between two pieces of card. Tie with one of the pieces of ribbon. Wrap the motto and hat round the present, secure with a rubber band and drop into the open end of the cracker. Squeeze and tie the second opening.

5 Tuck in any overlapping crepe paper to form a neat edge. Decorate with silver paper, extra ribbon, Christmas decorations from flower shops, etc.

If you prefer to use thin metallic paper or thin wrapping paper instead of crepe paper, you will not need lining paper.

Beeswax candles are exquisite, with their natural texture and delicious honey fragrance. For an unusual table decoration with beautiful reflections float flower-shaped candles in a shallow bowl of water.

Christmas Candles

Candles have been used in religious ceremonies for centuries. They are particularly associated with Christmas, a time when lighting fires, candles and special logs was a symbol of the renewal of life. In Estonia the custom of lighting candles on the graves of loved ones after the Christmas Eve service prevailed even while Christmas was banned under Soviet rule.

The Roman Catholic Church used to stipulate that candles were 100 per cent pure beeswax, but now the measure is down to only 25 per cent. There was a 10th-century Welsh law that Mass could only be said when bees were present, in the form of beeswax candles. Bees are holy because they swarmed out of Paradise in disgust at the Fall of Man.

Scottish Yule candles were much larger than ordinary ones and derive most probably from the torches of Scandinavian forbears. In the North of Scotland these were given to valued customers by shopkeepers at Christmas time – wax tapers were handed to the less prosperous.

In Norway, Christmas is a festival of lights, and candle-making was one of the annual and very necessary steps in preparation for Christmas – this job was often turned over to the oldest people on the farm. All fat from the slaughtering was saved. The tallow was melted and strained. Tallow from small animals made the finest candles – wicks were made of linen or hemp and they would turn out better if the weather was good. The way the candles burned on Christmas night presaged what would happen in the coming year.

In Germany, Poland and some other countries the lights on the Christmas tree are real candles, which are only lit on Christmas Eve.

A CHRISTMAS PROJECT

Making Your Own Rush Candles

In the days before electricity was widely available in rural areas, rush lights were the cheapest form of domestic lighting and the skills of the home chandler or candlemaker were highly esteemed. The rush 'taper' was mounted on a piece of bark and, unlike a wax candle, it did not drip.

You can still make your own rush candles by cutting soft rushes (*Juncus effusus* or *J. conglomeratus*) when they are fully grown but still green. Cut off the ends, peel away the green skin and hang the remaining rush up to dry.

Soak the dried rushes in a mixture of grease and beeswax. Mutton fat or the grease from boiling marrow bones is best. The beeswax makes the candles burn more brightly. Leave the rushes outside to dry hard. Repeat until they are well coated.

A PERSONAL REMINISCENCE

Christmas in Holland

Mrs G Dros of Den Burg writes:

When we were small (around 1920) we celebrated on Boxing Day in Sunday school. At about 5 o'clock we would go to the Reformed Church and there would stand a big pine tree, which they had collected from the woods. The tree was decorated with balls and thick white domestic candles, which were connected with a cotton fuse. Uncle Biem, an old man who sat on the council of the Sunday school for years, would dip those candles and the fuse in oil and would very carefully wrap the fuse around the candle with a loose knot. The candles and the fuse would then be fixed to the tree from top to bottom and from bottom to top.

When the Sunday school festivities began it was twilight, and that gave a very special atmosphere in the church. We would start singing Christmas carols and by the time we had finished some songs, it was dark outside. And then there was the big moment – I remember it so well. A big hand of a man lit the bottom of the fuse with a flickering light. The fire would lurch to the top of the tree and back until everything was lit – brilliant!

Decorating the Table

In Lithuania and Poland those anxious to preserve the old traditions spread a handful of fresh hay or straw on the table — a reminder that Jesus was born in a stable and laid in a manger. This is covered with a pure white table cloth and decorated with candles and sprays of fir. In Macedonia the meal table would be standing on straw, symbolising the manger, and next day the straw would be used around the fruit trees in the belief that it would ward off pests. In France, the Christmas table was covered with three white tablecloths and lit with three candles, symbolising the Trinity.

A CHRISTMAS PROJECT

Making Your Table Decoration

This elegant silver centrepiece with frosted fruit is easy to make and will look impressive on any table.

28cm/11in diameter ring of florists' foam (Oasis)
Additional blocks of Oasis to fill the centre of the ring
Sufficient dried leaves, seedheads and artificial or dried flowers to cover the Oasis generously — we used laurel leaves and an assortment of artificial flowers from a department store
A can of silver spray paint (optional)
3 or 4 limes and/or lemons and a bunch of white grapes
Beaten whites of 4 eggs
Enough caster sugar to cover the fruit
A pastry brush or small paintbrush
3 silver or white candles

1 Begin by frosting the fruit. Brush each item of fruit with egg white to make it sticky, then sprinkle with sugar. Don't worry about covering the entire fruit, as part of it will be hidden in the arrangement, and it doesn't matter it the odd bit of green or yellow shows through.

2 Arrange blocks of Oasis inside the ring to make a solid base, cutting them to the desired size with a sharp knife if necessary. You will achieve a better, tiered effect if the blocks are slightly higher than the rim.

3 Spray some or all of your flowers and leaves silver if you wish and leave for a few minutes to dry. Push the stem of a flower firmly into the Oasis, then add another very close to it and so on until you have covered the entire ring and some of the central blocks.

4 Press the frosted fruit firmly into the arrangement to fill most of the gaps. Leave room at the top for the candles.

5 Push the candles firmly into place and gently move the whole arrangement to the centre of the table.

Festive Food and Drink

In Britain, we are used to Christmas dinner being on Christmas Day, and turkey is now traditional, though in times past it was more likely to be beef or goose that was served. Other countries though have very different traditions, and for some, the main celebratory meal is held on Christmas Eve.

The Swedes just could not imagine the Christmas Eve feast without ham. Pork makes up a large proportion of Christmas fare and visitors often ask why the Swedes have to celebrate the birth of their Saviour by eating pig meat. The historical reason is that for a long time salt pork was the meat ration for the Swedes all the year round. The Christmas Eve meal starts with a special Smorgasbord followed by a whole ham flavoured with sugar and salt, coated with egg and bread crumbs, and boiled or roasted in the oven, usually served with some kind of cabbage. In some tradition-loving homes, the Smorgasbord is followed by lutfisk, this being a relic of the medieval fast, a meat-less fortnight when fresh fish was hard to come by. Dessert is often rice porridge served with warm milk and cinnamon. Today there are rituals that go with the rice pudding and whoever finds the hidden almond has to make up a 'porridge rhyme'. Cardamom bread and gingerbread cookies are served from St Lucia Day onwards (December 13th), throughout Christmas.

In Norway too pork is the usual main dish. It may be a whole roast piglet or served as pressed pork, roast pork with sour cabbage, smoked ham or pickled trotters. There are many kinds of small cakes, including the *Julekake* – the sweet Christmas

Glogg (see page 164)

bread filled with raisins, candied peel and cardamom. As in a number of European countries, gingerbread is a traditional item – the highlight of Christmas baking often being the amazing gingerbread house. After Norway's conversion to Christianity, the rulers wisely chose to give the old tradition regarding the sacrificial beer new symbolic meaning, rather than abolishing it. Beer was to be called Holiday Beer and according to one of the old laws of the land should be blessed on Christmas night, to Christ and the Virgin Mary.

Christmas dinner in Wales was often goose, and in some parts, a sumptuous goose pie was served. A boned roast goose was stuffed with a boiled chicken which contained an ox tongue. The whole was encased in pastry lined with minced meats, baked and eaten cold. This robust creation lasted the whole of Christmas week.

In Slovenia the main culinary event in the countryside before the Christmas period is the slaughter of a pig. The main purpose of slaughtering pigs at this particular time of the year is to provide quality meat dishes and other meat products for the rich Christmas table. The main Christmas meal therefore often contains homemade roast meat, various kinds of blood sausage and regular sausage filled with groats, boiled stuffed pig's stomach, and other delicacies.

On Christmas Day, the master of the house in Croatia did not go to Mass but stayed at home to roast the meat on a spit above the Yule log. The animal chosen was a young hog or sow, a lamb or goat-kid and the meat would be flavoured with rosemary.

In Germany goose with red cabbage is a traditional favourite. The significance of many of today's Christmas products dates back to the Middle Ages. This is particularly true of Christmas biscuits. In earlier times it was mainly the monasteries that produced special loaves and biscuits for the established Church festivals. *Dresdner Stollen* (fruit loaf), *Pfeffer Nusse* (ginger biscuit) and *Spekulatius* (almond biscuits) seem to be the most traditional.

For the Christmas feast in Greece, pigs are slaughtered from which sausages, brown and smoked ham are produced, while lamb is often cooked on a spit over a fire in a newly-dug pit, and this can occupy the men and the children with continually turning the handle. There are no such things as Christmas puddings but a large variety of small cakes are made, these being called *Christospsomi*, the most popular being Christmas Baclava.

In many Catholic countries the main dish on Christmas Eve is fish, since this is still a time of fasting. In the north of Portugal the main theme for Christmas Eve supper is salt cod, followed by octopus, while south of Lisbon the emphasis is definitely on meat, given that the pig-slaughter season is around this time of the year. Christmas lunch may start with a delicious mixture of all the salt cod dish left-overs, warmed up in olive oil strongly flavoured with garlic. This starter is nicknamed *roupa velha* (old clothes) denoting that it is something already used! Otherwise

Stuffed Turkey (see page 116)

the starter will be *canja*, a chicken broth soup slightly thickened with some rice or small pasta and garnished with chicken meat, some slices of *chouriço* (garlic sausage) that has been allowed to cook together with the rice or pasta, and a few mint leaves, freshly picked from the garden. It is a most comforting and tasty soup imaginable, and simplicity itself to make as are most Portuguese dishes. After the soup there may follow a fish dish or, more likely, meat. This can be turkey or a capon. *Bolo-Rei* (king's cake), which used to be reserved for the Epiphany, is now served from Christmas Day onwards and sometimes is available right up to Easter. *Bolo-Rei* is a ring, made with a yeast dough, filled with crystallised fruits and nuts. Inside there will be a small token wrapped up in paper, which brings good luck to the recipient – and a dried broad bean! Whoever finds this will have to supply the cake the following year. Desserts include *arroz doce*, the Portuguese version of rice pudding, which is not baked but made slowly on top of the stove and enriched with egg yolks, with plenty of cinnamon sprinkled on top before serving. *Sopa dourada*, golden soup, on account of its egg-yolk content, is another popular dessert as well as a variety of fried cakes, which are dipped in sugar and cinnamon, syrup or honey. As one would expect, port is served in abundance, either after the meals or between them, accompanying cakes. It will also be used as a night-cap, under the guise of mulled wine, especially after Midnight Mass.

Provence and Monaco also traditionally serve salt cod dishes on Christmas Eve, while in Slovakia and the Czech Republic carp is the favourite. In Poland they serve an assortment of fish – carp, pike and herrings, fried or marinated in oil or cream. The meal begins with borscht, and traditional Polish desserts are still the legendary poppyseed cake and a compote made from dried fruits.

In Gibraltar supper is taken late on Christmas Eve and consists mainly of a fruits-de-mer salad, followed by a main course of fried fish. In some homes on Boxing Day tripe is prepared with pigs' trotters, mint leaves, chick peas and Spanish sausage accompanied by a piquant sauce made with anchovies, almonds and pepper.

Apart from the traditional fish for the Christmas Eve feast, in Hungary over Christmas there is also the choice of pork or goose, with many kinds of sausage, black pudding, ham, Gulyas soup (goulash) and many kinds of pickle – onion, cabbage, gherkin. Hungarian pastries are ever present, but there is a special kind of Christmas cake (Beigli, see page 154)

Fruit soup (see page 141)

which consists of rolled pastry filled either with walnut or with poppy seed.

In Italy eels are very much associated with Christmas Eve. The menu for Christmas Day varies from region to region but is likely to include cappelletti filled with veal, chicken, ricotta and parmesan, and lamb baked in the oven on a bed of potatoes flavoured with garlic and rosemary. Cakes and desserts include panettone, torrone and panforte.

Although Iceland is a nation of fishermen, fish is absent from the Christmas celebrations. In most homes, smoked mutton is the main course of the special feast and is served with laufabraud – thin sheets of dough cut into intricate patterns and fried. Yule porridge is a traditional sweet and served to include the hidden, lucky almond! In past times, this was a delicacy in Iceland because of the scarcity of grain.

In Russia the many starters include caviar and pancakes with sour cream and little pies stuffed with cabbage, egg, beef, mushrooms, smoked salmon or dilled cucumber. There would be halibut or turbot in aspic with beetroot in vinegar, chicken paté, potato salad, aubergines, anchovies and stuffed eggs. Black and rye bread is served with unsalted butter. The main course is a choice between roast goose, or roast suckling pig served with apples, and accompanied by kasha – grains of various kinds, but very often buckwheat.

In Lithuania the principal dish on Christmas Eve used to be a mixture of various cooked grains – wheat, barley, oats, peas and beans. This mixture was called *Kucia* and was eaten with honey diluted with warm boiled water. The word itself comes from the Beylorussian and means a porridge of dried grain. Twelve different dishes – strictly meatless – are served at the table, because Jesus had twelve apostles: favourite choices are herring with poppy-seed milk, cranberry pudding, a dried fruit soup or compote, a winter salad with dried vegetables, mushrooms, boiled or baked potatoes, sauerkraut and special bread.

SPECIAL TRADITIONS

Christmas Pudding

An extract from The Christmas Almanac *by Michael Stephenson:*
Our Christmas pudding has its origins in a dish enjoyed in the Middle Ages by both rich and poor, the spicy porridge called frumenty. The first stage in making frumenty was to boil wheat in water until it turned into a soft porridge or gruel. To this was added milk, currants and other dried fruit. Then the yolks of eggs were mixed in, together with spices such as nutmeg and cinnamon. Finally, the frumenty mixture was cooked into a kind of stiff pudding.

Christmas pudding was, in fact, often called 'plum pottage', meaning a mixture as thick as porridge. Later it was sometimes called a 'hacker pudding' because the ingredients were chopped or hacked before going into the pudding.

After that it became the familiar plum pudding, although in the 19th century, instead of fresh plums, it only contained prunes, which are dried plums. Gradually the prunes gave way to other dried fruit, especially currants, sultanas and raisins.

Now that so many puddings come ready-made from supermarkets, we have almost lost one of our oldest and nicest of Christmas traditions. When Christmas puddings were made at home, silver charms and new coins were put into the mixture. Whoever found the charm in their piece of pudding would have good luck in the year to come.

The tradition dates right back to ancient Rome and the Saturnalia feast, when it was the custom to place a dried bean inside a cake. Whoever found the bean was 'king' for the evening, and permitted to order the other guests to make complete fools of themselves. This tradition continued with the Twelfth Night cake on January 6th, and lasted until almost the end of the Victorian age.

Bread

Bread has a particular significance at Christmas, and in many countries special loaves are baked only at this time. In Estonia it was a round or oblong loaf with a rough surface. On its top would be left the impression of a barn key, a brooch or a ring, or simply a fingerprint. The loaf was known as the Yule Hog, the New Year's bannock or winter's holiday bread.

In Cyprus special bread and pastries were prepared with a cross on the top and one of these would be hung from the beam in the ceiling and not taken down again until Christmas the following year. This was considered a good omen for the household. In Greece on every family table are loaves of *Christopsomo* (Christ bread) made in large, sweet loaves of various shapes, and the crusts are decorated in some way that reflects the family's profession. In country districts special bread is baked and comes in all shapes, with twists and other fanciful designs. This is called *Tsoureki*.

In Croatia the special loaf is round with pieces of dough plaited to make a cross, and a hole in the centre is made to hold a candle. In the Ukraine round braided bread is specially cooked and three of these loaves (*Kolachi*) are laid one on top of the other with a candle inserted in the centre of the top one. *Les Cougnous* is a type of bread eaten in Wallonia, especially in the Liège province, on Christmas Day. The bread is shaped like a baby and in shops will sometimes have the figure of a baby shaped in marzipan or sugar. In Provence the Christmas bread is called *fougasse*. It forms the centrepiece of the *treize* or thirteen desserts symbolizing Christ and his apostles. In Monaco the loaf of bread – *pain de Natale* – has four nuts forming a cross, surrounded by olive twigs.

A greatly respected tradition in Yugoslavia is the making of the sweet yeast flat bread ring, known as *Kolac* – circular with a hole in the middle. This loaf has to be ready for the midday meal on the same day as the Yule log is brought into the house and, before cooking, a little silver piece is hidden in the dough

which will bring luck to the finder. When baked, the *Kolac* is placed on a table beside a tall yellow candle, some straw, a glass of wine, an olive oil lamp and some nuts, apples and figs. A stalk of this straw is used to light the candle and after use is put back on the table. All these items remain in place all three days – and quite often until the New Year.

Mutual breaking and sharing of bread wafers, known as *Oplatek*, was and still is the very essence of Christmas Eve throughout Poland. In ancient times the family knelt on the floor to pray out loud together before this important ceremony. This is a time for deep feeling and the renewal of relationships. A piece of *Oplatek* sent in a letter to absent family members or friends brings much joy as a reminder of the Old Country and binds everyone together into one large family. There are many sayings about the popularity of bread in Poland: 'Bread unites the strongest', 'Bread cries when eaten for free'.

For the land where a crumb of bread

Is raised from the ground with reverence,

For the gifts of Heaven,

I Yearn, I Yearn, O Lord

SPECIAL TRADITIONS

Plum pudding

When the roast beef has been removed, when the pudding in all the glory of its splendour shines upon the table. How beautifully it steams! How delicious it smells! How round it is! A kiss is round, the horizon is round, the earth is round, the moon is round – so is plum pudding.   *The Illustrated London News 1848*

> How bless'd, how envied, were our life
> Could we but scape the poulterer's knife!
> But man, curs'd man, on Turkeys preys,
> And Christmas shortens all our days:
> Sometimes with oysters we combine,
> Sometimes assist the savoury chine;
> From the low peasant to the lord,
> The turkey smokes on every board.
> *From the fable 'The Turkey and the Ant' by John Gay (1685–1732)*

SPECIAL TRADITIONS

Receipt for Guernsey Mulled Wine

Some cloves and whole cinnamon;
An ounce of the last,
Of the first just one quarter;
Boiled, but not boiled too fast,
In a quart of cold water
To a dozen of wine;
Take a pound of loaf sugar,
Don't break it too fine;
Let them stand both together
While boiling the spice;
You can taste it to see
That the sweetness is nice.
And the cloves and the cinnamon
May simmer away,

If you're not in a hurry,
One third of the day;
it may then be poured into
The wine, and if fit
To be warmed – but not boiled
When you wish to drink it.

The Guernsey Rule: One coffee cup full of the Vin Brûlé to every young person. Two to married ladies, three – or at the utmost four – to each gentleman. More than this is an unlawful excess and disgraces the offender!

Christmas in Prison

An account by George Evatt, OBE, and Brita Brooks.

Although some prisoners in Dartmoor make a token effort to decorate their cells and landings, it is only in the chapel that you will find the traditional Christmas tree. Despite the fellowship and warmth that the chapel provides, very few prisoners avail themselves of it, or the church service on Christmas Day.

Christmas Day in prison is a day when the separation from loved ones is most keenly felt, and emotions run high. The predominant wish is for it to pass as quickly and with as little fuss as possible. With every endeavour being made to ensure that the majority of staff spends time with their families, the Christmas routine is reduced to eating and association.

Three things govern prison life – food, mail and visits. With only food available on Christmas Day, the catering officer plans through the year to make Christmas and New Year memorable. He scrimps and saves to ensure that the Christmas menu helps to sublimate the emotional feelings with gourmet satiation.

A TYPICAL DARTMOOR PRISON CHRISTMAS DAY MENU

Breakfast	**Dinner**	**Tea**	**Supper**
Grapefruit juice	Wholemeal roll, Asparagus soup	Hawaiian baked ham	Mincemeat pie
Weetabix x 2, milk	Sliced roast Norfolk turkey	Sliced corned beef	Packet of crisps
Fried Egg	Bacon and sausage olive	Sliced cheese	Fresh fruit
Fried Bread	Sage and onion stuffing		
Grilled Bacon	Roast potatoes and Gravy	**Vegetarians**	
Grilled Sausage	Croquette potatoes	Chutney	
Grilled tomato	Brussels sprouts	Sliced cheese x 2	
Toast & Marmalade	Vichy carrots	Coleslaw, beetroot Pasta salad	
		Russian salad	
Vegetarians	**Vegetarians**	Individual trifle	
Half grapefruit	Fresh trout	Slice of Christmas cake	
Vegetarian sausage	Buttered corn on cob		
	French onion rings		
	Ratatouille		

Green Bean Soup (Bou'neschlupp)

To add extra flavour, just before serving, some people like to add a chopped cooked Mettwurscht or sausage to each portion of this soup from Luxembourg.

Serves 4–6

Preparation time 15 minutes • Cooking time 30 minutes

❖ Melt the butter in a large saucepan, add the onions, potatoes and bacon and cook for 5 minutes, stirring occasionally.

❖ Add the green beans, stock and seasoning and stir to mix. Bring to the boil, then reduce the heat, cover and simmer for about 20 minutes or until the vegetables are tender, stirring occasionally.

❖ Stir in the cream and heat gently but do not boil. Adjust the seasoning, then ladle into warm soup bowls to serve. Serve topped with crispy croutons or with slices of fresh crusty bread.

25g/1oz butter
1 onion, finely chopped
225g/8oz potatoes, peeled and diced
4 rashers back bacon, diced
450g/1lb green beans, trimmed and sliced
1.2 litres/2 pints vegetable stock
salt and freshly ground black pepper
300ml/½ pint single cream

Variation

Use soured cream in place of single cream for an even more delicious flavour.

Mushrooms with Soured Cream

As in many parts of Europe, the most important meal of the Lithuanian Christmas is the Christmas Eve supper – known as Kucios – which marks the end of four weeks of fasting and preparation during Advent. This quick and easy dish can be served as a starter, but would traditionally have been one of the twelve dishes that made up the main course.

Serves 4–6

Preparation time 10 minutes • Cooking time 20 minutes

❖ Heat the oil in a pan, add the onions and cook for about 10 minutes or until softened but not brown, stirring occasionally.

❖ Add the mushrooms and cook for 5 minutes or until tender, stirring occasionally. Season to taste with salt and pepper.

❖ Stir in the sour cream and heat gently until warmed through, stirring, but do not allow the mixture to boil. Serve hot, with cooked potatoes or black rye bread.

2 tablespoons olive oil
2 large onions, finely chopped
900g/2lb closed cup or chestnut mushrooms, sliced
salt and freshly ground black pepper
125ml/4fl oz sour cream

Sweet Potato Turnovers

In the Algarve, sweet potatoes are very common and are used in all sorts of ways. The compote prepared as a filling for these turnovers is also good to eat by the spoonful on its own or used as a filling for tartlets.

Serves 4–6

Preparation time 55 minutes, plus kneading and resting time • Cooking time 15 minutes

❖ Cook the whole sweet potatoes in their skins in a saucepan of boiling water for about 20 minutes or until cooked and tender. Drain, cool slightly, then peel and discard the skins from the potatoes. Place the potatoes in a clean saucepan and mash until very smooth.

❖ Stir in the sugar and mix well. Add the cinnamon stick. Heat gently, stirring continuously, until the mixture slowly comes to the boil. Simmer gently until thick, stirring. Remove pan from the heat and discard the cinnamon stick. Set the potato mixture aside to cool.

❖ Mix the flour and salt in a bowl. Rub in the butter and lard, then make a well in the centre and add enough cold water, mixing to make a soft dough. On a lightly floured surface, knead the dough for 10 minutes. Place in a bowl, cover with a slightly damp cloth and leave to rest in a cool place for about 45 minutes.

❖ On a lightly floured surface, roll the dough out to a thickness of about 3mm/⅛in. Cut the dough into rounds about 10cm/4in in diameter. Place a spoonful of the sweet potato mixture in the centre of a round, fold in half and press the edges firmly together to seal. Repeat with the remaining dough rounds and sweet potato mixture.

❖ Heat the oil in a deep-fat fryer to 180°C/350°F. Add 2 or 3 turnovers and deep-fry for a few minutes or until golden brown and crisp. Drain on absorbent kitchen paper, then place on a warm plate and keep warm whilst cooking the remaining turnovers.

❖ Place the cooked turnovers on plates or in paper towels and sprinkle with a mixture of caster sugar and ground cinnamon. Serve warm or cold with a cup or mug of tea or coffee. These cooked turnovers are at their best if eaten fresh on the day they are made.

450g/1lb small sweet potatoes
250g/9oz granulated sugar
1 cinnamon stick
350g/12oz plain flour
pinch of salt
1 tablespoon butter
1 tablespoon lard
vegetable oil, for deep-frying
caster sugar and ground cinnamon, for
** sprinkling**

Tomates du Littoral

These tasty filled tomatoes from Belgium are simple to make and create an appetising starter or snack.

Serves 6   *Preparation time 20 minutes*

❖ Place the tomatoes in a bowl, cover with boiling water and leave for 30–60 seconds, then remove and plunge the tomatoes into a bowl of cold water. Drain, then peel off and discard the skins. Cut each tomato in half crossways and remove and discard the core and seeds. Set aside.

❖ Flake the fish finely and place in a bowl. Add the tomato puree, mustard, 2 teaspoons mayonnaise and seasoning and mix well.

❖ Season the tomato cups and fill each one generously with the fish mixture. Place half a teaspoon of the remaining mayonnaise on top of each filled tomato cup and cover with prawns. Serve on a bed of watercress, accompanied by thick slices of country bread.

6 large tomatoes
500g/1lb 2oz cooked white fish fillet,
** such as cod or haddock**
2 teaspoons tomato puree
2 teaspoons French or Dijon mustard
8 teaspoons mayonnaise
salt and freshly ground black pepper
115g/4oz cooked, peeled prawns

a handful of watercress or other green
** leaves, to serve**

Dry Salt Cod (Bakalar za Badnjak)

The traditional Croatian way of cooking bakalar *is with potatoes. It can be prepared in advance and reheated when needed. This is a simple and delicious recipe traditionally served on Christmas Eve.*

Serves 4

Preparation time 25 minutes, plus soaking time • Cooking time 40 minutes

❖ Place the cod in a large bowl and cover with plenty of cold water. Leave overnight or even longer, changing the water at least twice. Drain.

❖ Place the fish in a saucepan with the peppercorns and bay leaves and cover with boiling water. Bring gently to the boil, then poach or simmer gently for about 20 minutes or until tender. Remove the fish from the water (stock) using a slotted spoon and place on a plate. Set aside to cool slightly. Strain and reserve the fish stock, discarding the peppercorns and bay leaves.

❖ Peel and thickly slice the potatoes and cook them in a saucepan in some of the boiling fish stock for about 15 minutes or until cooked and tender. Drain the potatoes.

❖ Meanwhile, remove and discard the skin and bones from the fish and flake the flesh.
❖ Place the fish in a saucepan away from the heat. Chop the garlic and parsley and add to the fish with some ground black pepper. Slowly add the oil and a little of the fish stock, if necessary, stirring continuously.

❖ Cover the saucepan, hold the lid on firmly and shake the pan vigorously until the fish mixture becomes milky in appearance. Add the cooked potatoes and shake everything together. Reheat gently, shaking the pan occasionally, then adjust the seasoning to taste and serve. Serve with fresh crusty bread.

500g/1lb 2oz salt cod
a few whole black peppercorns
2 bay leaves
1kg/2lb 4oz potatoes
4–5 cloves garlic, peeled
handful of fresh parsley
freshly ground black pepper
125ml/4fl oz virgin olive oil

Salted Cod Cakes

Salted cod cakes are one of the most delicious and popular dishes in Portugal. They are eaten all year round, including at Christmas and can be served hot or cold, on the same day or on the following day. These fish cakes are also picnic fare par excellence and everybody (even those who think they will not be able to eat salt cod) adores them. They are often served as an introduction to salted cod dishes outside Portugal or to foreign visitors to the country.

Serves 4

Preparation time 30 minutes, plus soaking time • Cooking time 10–15 minutes

❖ Place the cod in a bowl, cover with plenty of cold water and leave to soak overnight, changing the water several times. Drain.

❖ Place the cod in a pan and add just enough water to cover. Bring to the boil, reduce the heat and poach gently for about 15 minutes, or until the fish is cooked and flakes easily. Remove the fish from the pan and place on a plate. Meanwhile, heat the olive oil in a pan, add the onion and cook until softened, stirring occasionally.

❖ At the same time, cook the potatoes in a saucepan of lightly salted, boiling water for 10–15 minutes, or until cooked and tender. Drain well and mash until smooth, then add the onion and parsley and mix well.

❖ Remove and discard any bones and skin from the fish and flake the fish very finely until it resembles threads (this is best done by rubbing the fish inside a clean cloth). Add the flaked fish to the mashed potato mixture and mix well. Add beaten egg to the potato mash if necessary, mixing to make a soft but not sloppy mixture. Season to taste (although check the seasoning first as you may not need to add any salt).

❖ Using lightly floured hands, shape the mixture into 8 flat, round cakes. Brush each one with beaten egg and coat with breadcrumbs. Heat a little vegetable oil in a frying pan, add the fish cakes and fry, turning once, until crisp and golden brown all over. Drain on absorbent kitchen paper and serve. Serve hot or cold with roast vegetables such as roast potatoes, peppers and courgettes.

300g/10½oz thick salt cod, sliced
1 tablespoon olive oil
1 small onion, finely chopped
400g/14oz floury potatoes, diced
2 tablespoons chopped fresh parsley
beaten egg, to bind and for brushing
salt and freshly ground black pepper
dried or fresh breadcrumbs, for coating
vegetable oil, for shallow frying

Glass Masters Herring

These traditional Finnish herrings will keep for a couple of weeks in a cool place but are at their best after 4–5 days.

Serves 6–8

Preparation time 30 minutes, plus soaking and marinating time Cooking time 10 minutes

❖ Place the fish in a large bowl and cover with cold water. Leave to soak overnight, changing the water twice.

❖ Meanwhile, prepare the marinade. Place the vinegar and sugar in a saucepan with 600ml/1 pint water. Heat gently, stirring, until the sugar has dissolved, then bring to the boil. Remove the pan from the heat and leave to cool. Drain the fish, dry with absorbent kitchen paper and cut into slices.

❖ Fill a large glass jar with alternate layers of fish slices, onions, carrots, allspice berries, peppercorns and bay leaves, until all the ingredients are used up. Pour over the cooled marinade. Seal the jar and store in a cool place for at least 2 days before serving with thick slices of buttered fresh bread.

4 good-sized herrings, each about 225–280g/8–10oz, gutted, trimmed and cleaned
300ml/½ pint white wine vinegar
250g/9oz granulated sugar
3 red onions, sliced into rings
2 carrots, sliced
30 whole dried allspice berries
30 whole white peppercorns
4 bay leaves

Variations

Different spices such as thin slices of fresh horseradish, celery seeds or mustard seeds can be used instead of the above spices. To save some time, the fish can also be filleted and the skin removed. Pre-soaking in water is then not required.

Stuffed Fish Fillets

Another Lithuanian speciality, these tasty fish fillets are a traditional part of the Christmas Eve supper.

Serves 4   *Preparation time 25 minutes • Cooking time 30–35 minutes*

❖ Preheat the oven to 170°C/325°F/Gas Mark 3. Heat the oil in a pan, add the onions and mushrooms and cook for about 10 minutes until softened, stirring occasionally. Add 55g//2oz breadcrumbs, the parsley and seasoning and mix well. Stir in 3–4 tablespoons of stock.

❖ Place the fish fillets on a chopping board and divide the onion mixture evenly between each fillet. Spread the filling over each fish fillet, roll up and tie with string. Sprinkle the fish rolls with the remaining breadcrumbs.

❖ Place the fish in a lightly greased ovenproof dish, cover and bake in the oven for 20 minutes. Uncover and pour the remaining fish stock and the wine over the fish. Increase the oven temperature to 180°C/350°F/Gas Mark 4 and bake for a further 10–15 minutes, or until the fish is cooked. Cool slightly, carefully remove and discard the string, then serve the fish while still warm. Serve with cooked seasonal fresh vegetables such as potatoes, green beans and carrots.

3 tablespoons olive oil
1 onion, finely chopped
115g/4oz mushrooms, finely chopped
85g/3oz dry breadcrumbs
1 tablespoon chopped fresh parsley
salt and freshly ground white pepper
125ml/4fl oz hot fish stock
4 white fish fillets such as cod or haddock, each weighing about 200g/7oz
125ml/4fl oz dry white win

Freshly Salted Salmon with Mustard Dressing ·

An important Christmas delicacy for many Finns is the special cod dish known as Lute Fish *or* Lipeakala. *The traditional recipe involves soaking the fish in cold water which is changed every day for a week, then covering it with a 'soup' made from cooking birch ashes and soaking for a further week.*

Most people now prefer to buy Lute Fish ready-made from the supermarket, but this salted salmon can easily be prepared at home. It is delicious on its own, but the mustard dressing goes very well with it if you prefer a moister dish.

Serves 8–10

Preparation time 25 minutes, plus 1–2 days salting time

❖ Fillet the salmon into two large pieces but do not remove the skin. Wipe with absorbent kitchen paper without rinsing.

❖ Sprinkle the bottom of a non-metallic dish with half the sea salt and place one of the fillets, skin side down, on the salt. Mix the sugar and white pepper together and spread over both the fillets (on the skinless side). Place the other fillet on top of the first, skin side up.

❖ Sprinkle with the remaining salt and then sprinkle the dill over the top. Cover the dish tightly with foil. Place a small weight on top and store in a cool place for 1–2 days.

❖ Make the mustard dressing. Mix together the mustard, sugar and wine vinegar. Gradually whisk in the oil, pouring it in slowly in a thin stream and whisking continuously. Stir in the dill. Cover and set aside until ready to serve.

❖ Scrape all the seasoning off the salmon and cut the fillets down to the skin in thin, oblique slices. Serve the salted salmon with the mustard dressing. Serve with buttered fresh brown bread.

For the salted salmon:
a large piece of salmon about 2kg/4½lb in weight
2 tablespoons coarse sea salt
2 tablespoons caster sugar
1 tablespoon roughly ground white pepper
3 tablespoons chopped fresh dill

For the mustard dressing:
3 tablespoons dark prepared mustard such as French or Dijon mustard
2 tablespoons caster sugar
4 tablespoons white wine vinegar
175ml/6fl oz olive oil
3–4 tablespoons chopped fresh dill

FISH IN LUXEMBOURG

In Luxembourg, the Christmas meal is based on traditional dishes from neighbouring France and Germany. The Christmas Eve Réveillon often features game dishes such as civet or venison, but Luxembourg also boasts a number of delicious fish dishes, which are the best accompaniments to the beautiful white wines such as dry Riesling or Elbling. Luxembourgers say that fish should always swim – first in water, then in hot fat, and lastly in good wine. These popular recipes bear out that principle!

Trout in Riesling Sauce
(F'rell Am Reisleck)

Serves 4   *Preparation time 20 minutes • Cooking time 20–25 minutes*

❖ Preheat the oven to 200°C/400°F/Gas Mark 6. Lightly grease a flameproof, ovenproof dish and set aside. Gut, clean and wash the trout, then dry with absorbent kitchen paper. Sprinkle each trout with salt, pepper and flour.

❖ Melt the butter in a frying pan, add the trout and fry gently for 2–3 minutes on each side. Remove from the pan using a slotted spoon and place in the prepared dish. Set aside.

❖ Add the shallots and chopped herbs to the frying pan with the Riesling wine. Bring to the boil, stirring. Stir in the cream and season with salt, pepper and paprika. Heat until hot, then pour this mixture over the trout.

❖ Cover and bake in the oven for 15–20 minutes, or until the trout are cooked and tender, basting the trout once or twice.

❖ Remove the trout from the dish using a slotted spoon and place on a warm plate. Cover and keep warm. Boil the sauce on the hob, whisking continuously, until the sauce reduces and thickens.

❖ Pour the sauce over the trout and serve immediately with boiled potatoes and cooked fresh vegetables such as broccoli and cauliflower florets.

4 whole trout, each about 225g/8oz
salt and freshly ground black pepper
plain flour, for sprinkling
55g/2oz unsalted butter
3 shallots, finely chopped
1 tablespoon finely chopped fresh
**   parsley**
1 tablespoon chopped fresh chives
sprig of fresh tarragon, finely chopped
pinch of chopped fresh chervil
200ml/7fl oz dry Riesling wine
300ml/½ pint double cream
pinch of paprika

Friture de la Moselle

Serves 4   *Preparation time 45 minutes • Cooking time 10–15 minutes*

❖ Descale the fish. This is done by holding the tail fin and scraping the fish with a short, not too sharp knife, in the direction of the head. With a very sharp knife, slit the length of the belly of each fish and remove and discard the entrails. Rinse well and dry using absorbent kitchen paper.

❖ Season the fish with salt and pepper and place in a bowl. Pour over the lemon juice and toss the fish to ensure they are coated thoroughly.

approx. 60 very small herring or sprat,
**   about 700g/1lb 9oz in total weight**
salt and freshly ground white pepper
juice of 4 lemons
plain flour, for coating
vegetable oil, for deep-frying

chopped fresh parsley and lemon
**   slices, to garnish**

Cook's Tip
Use whitebait if small herring or sprat are not available.

◈   Place some flour in a bowl and dip each fish into the flour until thoroughly coated all over.

◈   Heat the oil in a deep-fat fryer to 180°C/350°F. Add the fish in batches and deep-fry for a few minutes or until cooked, golden brown and crisp. Drain on absorbent kitchen paper, then place on a warm plate and keep hot whilst cooking the remaining fish.

◈   Garnish with chopped parsley and lemon slices and serve immediately. As 'Friture' are traditionally eaten with fingers, it is wise to supply guests with a bowl of fresh lemon water for washing their hands.

Mussels Luxembourg Style

This hugely popular dish should be served with pommes frites and a glass or two of outstanding Riesling.

Serves 4

Preparation time 30 minutes • Cooking time 35 minutes

◈   Melt 55g/2oz butter in a large saucepan, add the onions and shallots and fry gently until lightly browned, stirring occasionally. Add the leeks, carrot, celery, celery leaves, thyme and tarragon and mix well. Stir in 100ml/3½fl oz of the Riesling wine, bring to the boil, then reduce the heat and simmer for 15 minutes.

◈   Meanwhile, peel and crush the garlic and mix with the remaining butter. Season with a little black pepper. Set aside.

◈   Add the remaining wine to the saucepan and cook over a high heat until boiling. Drop the mussels into the boiling liquid, then cover firmly with a lid and continue to cook. Every couple of minutes, stir with a circular movement to make sure the mussels do not remain at the bottom of the pan.

◈   After about 10 minutes, all the mussels should have opened. Now add the garlic butter to the pan and in 2–3 minutes, with regular stirring, the sauce should have mixed thoroughly. Adjust the seasoning, sprinkle with chopped parsley and serve immediately. Serve with crisp pommes frites.

150g/5½oz butter, softened
1 onion, finely chopped
2 shallots, finely chopped
2 leeks, washed and finely chopped
1 carrot, finely chopped
1 large stick celery and a few celery
   leaves, finely chopped
a sprig of fresh thyme, finely chopped
2 fresh tarragon leaves, finely chopped
400ml/14fl oz Riesling wine
5 cloves garlic
salt and freshly ground black pepper
3kg/6½lb cleaned mussels

chopped fresh parsley, to garnish

Cook's Tip

Mussels are always served with pommes frites, both of which are best eaten with the fingers. Do not forget to place an empty dish on the table for the discarded shells. Experienced mussel-eaters slide the empty shells into one another – this takes up less space and no one can tell how many you have eaten!

Stuffed Turkey (Tacchino Ripieno Di Natale)

The stuffing in this Sicilian recipe combines many flavours and creates a delicious stuffed turkey, oven-roast with onions and potatoes, that is sure to impress family and friends.

Serves 10–12

Preparation time 40 minutes • Cooking time 3½–4 hours

❖ Preheat the oven to 190°C/375°F/Gas Mark 5. Bone the turkey and set aside. Place the minced veal, breadcrumbs, parmesan cheese, 2 raw eggs, salt, pepper and parsley in a bowl and mix well.

❖ Shell the hard-boiled eggs and chop them, then add to the veal mixture with the bacon and ham and mix well. Add enough water, mixing to make a soft mixture. Stuff the turkey with this mixture, making sure the legs are also stuffed. Truss or secure the turkey loosely with string, reshaping the bird. Weigh the bird, then place it in a large roasting tin.

❖ Spread lard all over the turkey and season with salt and pepper. Roast in the oven, allowing about 25 minutes per 450g/1lb or about 55 minutes per 1kg/2lb 4oz, basting and turning occasionally. After about 1½ hours, place the sliced onions in the roasting tin around the turkey. After a further 1 hour, place the potatoes in the roasting tin around the turkey.

❖ Make sure the turkey and stuffing are thoroughly cooked before serving. If the bird shows signs of browning too quickly, cover it with a piece of foil. Serve the hot stuffed turkey in slices with the roast onions and potatoes. Serve with additional cooked fresh vegetables such as green beans and roast peppers.

1 medium-sized turkey, about
    3.6–4.5kg/8–10lb in weight
500g/1lb 2oz minced veal
150g/5½oz fresh breadcrumbs
150g/5½oz parmesan cheese, grated
2 medium eggs
salt and freshly ground black pepper
3 tablespoons chopped fresh parsley
4 hard-boiled medium eggs, cooled
300g/10½oz bacon, finely chopped
300g/10½oz uncooked ham, finely
    chopped
lard, for roasting
3 onions, sliced
2kg/4½lb potatoes, peeled and cut
    into even-sized pieces

Goose with Apples and Prunes

This delicious Danish roast goose with all the trimmings is ideal for a gathering of family and friends at Christmas. This recipe was generously contributed by HRH the Duchess of Gloucester.

Serves 10   *Preparation time 45 minutes • Cooking time 7 hours*

❖   Wash and dry the goose. Cut off wings and reserve for the sauce. Smear butter inside the goose and season with salt and pepper. Rinse, core and quarter apples, leaving the peel on. Put the apples and prunes inside the goose and in skin of the neck. Sew ends of the goose together.

❖   Place the goose on its back in a large roasting tin, in a cold oven, then turn the oven on to 170°C/325°F/Gas Mark 3. Roast for 45 minutes, then pour the fat from the tin into a bowl. Pour the simmering chicken stock into the roasting tin and return the goose to the oven on the lowest shelf. Roast for a further 2½–3 hours, covering with foil if it begins to brown too quickly. If the liquid beneath the goose is about to dry up, add some more water.

❖   Meanwhile, cut the neck into two and rinse it with the wings, gizzard and heart. Drain and dry on kitchen paper. Cut the gizzard and heart into small pieces. Melt the butter in a saucepan, add the neck, wings, gizzard and heart and fry until browned all over, stirring occasionally. Stir in 100ml/3½fl oz of the Marsala wine and bring to the boil. Boil for 2 minutes, then add the chicken stock. Bring back to the boil, cover, reduce the heat and simmer for about 45 minutes.

❖   Strain the sauce through a sieve, discarding the contents of the sieve. Return sauce to a clean pan and boil rapidly for 10 minutes to reduce slightly and intensify the flavour. Set aside.

❖   Turn the goose over and pour some boiling water into the roasting tin if it is about to dry up. Continue roasting for a further 3 hours, adding extra water if necessary. About 30 minutes before the goose has finished cooking, pour the cooking juices into a bowl and then return the goose to the oven. Remove the fat from the cooking juices and save 50ml/2fl oz of fat for the sauce. Place the rest of the fat in a bowl and set aside.

❖   Remove the goose from the oven and place on a large dish. Cover with foil and some clean towels to keep it warm. Let the goose rest for about 30 minutes before carving.

❖   Meanwhile, sieve the juices from the roasting tin and add to the sauce made earlier. Bring to the boil and boil for about 10 minutes until the taste is strong, stirring occasionally. Mix the reserved 50ml/2fl oz goose fat with the flour and gradually whisk this into the boiling sauce. Boil for a further 2 minutes, whisking, then pour the remaining 100ml/3½fl oz Marsala wine and the cream into the sauce. Bring to the boil, stirring, then simmer for 3–4 minutes. Season to taste with salt and pepper. Serve the goose with the sauce and the fruit from inside the bird.

For the goose:

7kg/15½lb goose
25g/1oz butter, softened
salt and freshly ground black pepper
700g/1lb 9oz dessert apples
400g/14oz pitted prunes
1.2 litres/2 pints hot chicken stock

For the sauce:

neck, wings, gizzard and heart from
   goose
25g/1oz butter
200ml/7fl oz dry Masala wine
1 litre/1¾ pints hot chicken stock
7 tablespoons plain flour
500ml/18fl oz double cream

Cook's Tips

Once the cooked goose has rested, the goose can be put in a very hot oven at 240°C/475°F/Gas Mark 9 for a few minutes just before serving, to make the skin extra crispy.

Store the leftover goose fat in a covered container in a cool place. In Denmark, the remaining goose fat is used for the Christmas lunches that follow Christmas Eve. The fat is spread on black bread and is topped with herrings, meat or pate to make an open sandwich which is the most important part of a traditional Danish lunch.

Spiced Beef

This recipe for spiced beef is a popular dish in Northern Ireland at Christmas time, not instead of turkey or goose, but as an extra over the days around Christmas.

Serves 20

Preparation time 15 minutes, plus rubbing and turning for 14 days • Cooking time 4 hours

❖ In a bowl, mix the sugar, saltpetre, white pepper, nutmeg, cloves, mace and cayenne pepper together. Rub this mixture all over the beef. Place the beef in a dish, sprinkle over any leftover sugar and spice mixture, cover and leave in a cool place.

❖ Each day, for 3 days, turn and rub the beef with the sugar and spice mixture, then cover again and leave in a cool place.

On day 4, sprinkle the salt over the beef and rub it in. Cover and leave in a cool place. Continue to turn and rub the salt and spice mixture into the meat, as before, for the next 10 days. On day 14, rinse the beef under cold running water and drain. Discard any leftover salt and spice mixture.

Place the beef in a large pan, cover with plenty of water and bring to the boil. Reduce the heat, cover and simmer the beef slowly for 4 hours, or until cooked and tender. Remove from the pan and set aside to cool before slicing. Serve in slices with Cumberland sauce.

350g/12oz granulated sugar
25g/1oz saltpetre or sodium nitrate (preservative, available from chemists and kosher butchers)
4 teaspoons ground white pepper
3 teaspoons ground nutmeg
2 teaspoons ground cloves
½ teaspoon ground mace
¼ teaspoon cayenne pepper
3.6kg/8lb piece of rolled rib of beef, topside or silverside
350g/12oz salt

Braised Beef

Although in the northern part of Portugal fish is traditionally eaten on Christmas Eve, meat dishes predominate to the south of Lisbon and in some of the Portuguese islands, including Madeira and the Azores. The Christmas Eve supper is called Consoada, *which means 'something done together' – a perfect title for an occasion shared with family and friends.*

Serves 6–8

Preparation time 20 minutes, plus marinating time • Cooking time 3–3½ hours

Spread the lard all over the beef and sprinkle with the peppercorns. Place the beef in a non-metallic dish and pour over the Madeira or port and vinegar. Sprinkle with a little salt. Cover and set aside to marinate in a cool place for 4 hours, turning the beef over in the marinade several times.

Remove the beef from the marinade and reserve the marinade. Heat the oil in a large saucepan, add the beef and fry until well-sealed all over and golden brown, turning frequently.

Add the bay leaf, reserved marinade and the stock. Cover, bring to the boil, then reduce the heat and simmer for 1½ hours. Turn the beef over, add the whole tomato and onion (added to give flavour), cover the pan and simmer for a further 1½–2 hours, or until the beef is cooked and tender.

Remove and discard the tomato, onion, peppercorn and bayleaf and add the potatoes to the pan. Cover and continue simmering, until the potatoes are cooked and tender. Adjust the seasoning.

Serve the braised beef in slices with the sauce poured over. Serve with the cooked potatoes alongside and scatter the beef with a few olives just before serving.

1 tablespoon lard
1.5kg/3lb 5oz roasting beef joint such as topside
10 black peppercorns
150ml/¼ pint Madeira or port
1 tablespoon red or white wine vinegar
salt and freshly ground black pepper
3 tablespoons olive oil
1 bay leaf
600ml/1 pint hot beef stock
1 slightly unripe tomato
1 onion, peeled
1kg/2lb 4oz new potatoes, cut into small even-sized chunks

black or green olives, to garnish

Cook's Tips

If desired, the sauce can be thickened before serving. Simply place the cooked beef and potatoes on a serving platter and keep warm. Blend 3 tablespoons cornflour with a little water, add to the juices in the pan, bring to the boil, stirring continuously, simmer for 3 minutes, stirring, then pour over beef to serve.

Smoked Collar of Pork (Judd Mat Gaardebou'nen)

*This dish has come to be regarded as the national dish of Luxembourg and hails
from the village of Gostingen. The villagers there have often disparagingly been called
'Bou'nepatscherten' – 'bean cooks' – by their neighbours, who are jealous of the fact
that the best broad beans are grown in the area. Indeed these are celebrated annually
in a 'Bean Feast'.*

Serves 4–6

Preparation time 15 minutes, plus overnight soaking time
Cooking time 2–2½ hours

❖ Place the pork in a large saucepan, cover with water and leave to soak for 24
hours. Bring to the boil in the same water, then reduce the heat and simmer for 30
minutes. Drain and discard the water and cover the pork again with fresh water.

❖ Bring to the boil again, reduce the heat, cover and simmer for 1½–2 hours or
until the pork is cooked and tender, adding the prepared vegetables to the pan for the
last 30 minutes of the cooking time.

❖ Meanwhile, make the bean sauce. Cook the broad beans in a pan of lightly
salted, boiling water for 8–10 minutes or until tender. Drain and keep warm. In the
meantime, melt the butter in a pan, add the onion and bacon and cook gently for 10
minutes, stirring occasionally. Add the flour and cook for 1 minute, stirring, then
gradually stir in the stock.

❖ Bring to the boil, stirring continuously, until the sauce comes to the boil and
thickens. Simmer for 2–3 minutes, stirring. Stir in the cooked broad beans, chopped
herbs, cream and seasoning and reheat gently before serving, stirring.

❖ Serve the cooked pork in slices with the vegetables alongside and the bean sauce
spooned over.

For the pork:

1.3kg/3lb smoked collar of pork
450g/1lb baby new potatoes
225g/8oz carrots, sliced
225g/8oz parsnips, cut into chunks
225g/8oz shallots

For the broad beans:

450g/1lb shelled fresh or frozen broad
    beans
salt and freshly ground black pepper
25g/1oz butter
1 onion, chopped
2 rashers streaky bacon, diced
25g/1oz plain flour
300ml/½ pint vegetable stock
2 teaspoons chopped fresh savoury
1–2 tablespoons chopped fresh
    parsley
4 tablespoons double cream

Ham in Hay (Haam am Hee)

*This recipe comes from the very north of Luxembourg. Reduce the size of the ham
and water used to suit your requirements – 1kg /2lb 4oz ham joint will serve
approximately 6 people.*

Serves 16–20   *Preparation time 10 minutes • Cooking time 3–4 hours*

Take a very large metal pan and part fill it with hay. Add 3–5 litres/5¼–8¾ pints of water over the hay. Lay the ham on the hay in such a manner that it does not touch the water, so that it is cooking by steaming. If necessary, add extra hay during the cooking process.

Cover the pan and bring to the boil. Reduce the heat and simmer, allowing 20–25 minutes per 450g/1lb or 45–55 minutes per 1kg/2lb 4oz, until the ham is tender. From time to time, top up the water if necessary, to replace the water that has evaporated. Serve the cooked ham on a bed of hay with pomme frites and a mixed salad.

clean hay, for cooking and serving
1 lightly smoked shoulder of ham, about 4kg/9lb in weight, rinsed

Baked Ham

This Finnish Christmas meal is full of unique smells and tastes, with many of the dishes being prepared only for this one meal of the year. This recipe is delicious served hot or cold.

4.5kg/10lb ready-salted ham
2 tablespoons mustard
2 tablespoons soft light brown sugar
2 tablespoons dried breadcrumbs

whole cloves, to garnish

Serves 20 • *Preparation time 10 minutes* • *Cooking time 3½–4 hours*

Preheat the oven to 170°C/325°F/Gas Mark 3. Place the ham, skin side up, on a wire rack in a roasting tin. Push a roasting thermometer into the thickest part of the ham making sure it does not touch the bone.

Calculate the cooking time allowing 20 minutes per 450g/1lb, plus 20 minutes, or 45 minutes per 1kg/2lb 4oz, plus 20 minutes. It is difficult to give a precise roasting time and it is best to go by the roasting thermometer. Put the ham in the oven and roast for the calculated time or until the thermometer reaches 77°C/170°F and the meat is cooked.

Remove the ham from the oven and let it stand for a few minutes. Remove and discard as much of the skin and underlying fat as you can. Increase the oven temperature to 230°C/450°F/Gas Mark 8.

Mix together the mustard, sugar and breadcrumbs and smear this mixture over the ham. Return the ham to the oven and bake for 10–15 minutes, or until golden brown all over. Garnish the surface of the ham with whole cloves. Serve the baked ham hot or cold, carved into slices. Serve with cooked seasonal fresh vegetables such as boiled potatoes, carrots and celery.

Cook's Tips

If the ham is cooked at a lower temperature, less liquid will be lost and the meat will be more succulent. However, remember that the lower the cooking temperature, the longer the cooking time.

The meat juices which collect in the roasting tin can be used to make a tasty gravy. Be careful, however, as it will be rather salty. One well-tried method is to mix in some apple sauce and flavour with ground ginger and mustard. Serve with the warm ham.

A POLISH FEAST

The most important meal of the Polish Christmas has always been the Christmas Eve supper, the last meal of the period of fasting that precedes Christmas Day. In this context 'fasting' means eating no meat and, in the strictest Catholic homes, preparing food with oil rather than animal fat.

In wealthy homes and in the monasteries, the Christmas Eve supper traditionally consisted of twelve dishes – one for each of the twelve Apostles. In the absence of meat, fish dishes, especially carp, had pride of place. In fact, there are so many traditional ways of preparing fish for this meal that it can be difficult to limit the number of dishes to twelve. An ingenious solution to this problem is to count all the fish dishes together as one course.

The following are just a few of the traditional Polish Christmas Eve dishes.

Almond Soup (Zupa migdalowa)

Serves 6   *Preparation time 25 minutes • Cooking time 20 minutes*

❖ Cook the rice in a saucepan of boiling water for 10–12 minutes, or until tender. Drain and rinse the rice with boiling water, then drain again and set aside.

❖ Meanwhile, place the almonds in a saucepan and cover with cold water. Bring to the boil, then pour into a sieve to drain. While the nuts are still warm, peel off and discard the skins.

❖ Place the peeled almonds in a blender or food processor, add 150ml/¼ pint milk and blend until relatively smooth. Set aside.

❖ Heat the remaining milk and sugar in a saucepan over a gentle heat until almost boiling, stirring occasionally to dissolve the sugar. Stir in the cooked rice, ground almonds, almond extract or essence and raisins and heat gently until hot, stirring occasionally. Ladle into warm soup bowls and serve.

100g/3½oz long grain white rice
225g/8oz whole unpeeled almonds
litres/2¼ pints milk
50g/1¾oz caster sugar
1 teaspoon almond extract or essence
85g/3oz raisins

Bortsch

Serves 4–6   *Preparation time 25 minutes • Cooking time 40 minutes*

❖ Place the beetroot, onions, celeriac, carrots, leeks, parsley stalks, bay leaf, allspice, pepper and stock in a large saucepan and bring to the boil. Cover, reduce the heat and simmer for about 30 minutes, or until the vegetables are tender, stirring occasionally.

❖ Meanwhile, place the rehydrated mushrooms in a separate saucepan and add 450ml/16fl oz water. Bring to the boil, cover, then reduce the heat and simmer for 20 minutes.

❖ Strain the vegetables and stock through a sieve and reserve the stock. Discard the vegetables. Strain the mushrooms through a sieve, reserve the cooking liquid and discard the mushrooms (the mushrooms can be used in the Pierozki recipe). Mix the vegetable and mushroom stocks together and return to a rinsed-out pan.

❖ Add the soured beet juice (about 425ml/¾ pint beet juice to 1.4 litres/2½ pints stock) and garlic. Heat the borsch gently until it comes to the boil, stirring occasionally. If the colour of the borsch is not right, add 1 raw beetroot, coarsely grated, to the soup and stir to mix.

❖ Adjust the seasoning, adding salt to taste. Ladle into warm soup bowls to serve.

4 raw beetroot, peeled and thinly sliced
1 onion, chopped
225g/8oz celeriac, peeled and diced
2 carrots, chopped
2 leeks, washed and sliced
small bunch of fresh parsley stalks
1 bay leaf
¼ teaspoon ground allspice
salt and freshly ground black pepper
1.4 litres/2½ pints vegetable stock
85g/3oz dried boletus mushrooms,
**   soaked in warm water and drained**
about 425ml/¾ pint soured beet juice
**   (see Cook's Tip, below)**
1 clove garlic, crushed

Cook's Tips

The bortsch should be flavoured very carefully and its final flavour depends on individual preferences. Apart from salt, the taste may also be corrected with the addition of a little sugar. The acidity may be enhanced with a glass of dry red wine or lemon juice but never with vinegar. The addition of the crushed garlic gives the bortsch an interesting taste and aroma.

Pierozki

These can be made in advance and reheated just before serving.

Serves 4–6

Preparation time 50 minutes • Cooking time 10–15 minutes

❖ Lightly grease a baking sheet and set aside. Make the dough. Mix the flour and salt in a bowl, then rub in the butter. Add the small egg or egg yolks and sour cream and mix to form a soft dough. Knead lightly, then place in a bowl, cover and leave to rest in a cool place for about 30 minutes.

❖ Meanwhile make the mushroom farce. Place the rehydrated mushrooms in a saucepan and add 450ml/16fl oz boiling water. Bring to the boil, cover, then reduce the heat and simmer for 20 minutes. Drain, reserving the mushrooms. The stock may also be reserved for use in the Bortsch recipe.

❖ Preheat the oven to 200°C/400°F/Gas Mark 6. Dice the cooked mushrooms very finely. Melt the butter in a frying pan, add the onions and mushrooms and cook for about 5 minutes, or until the onion is softened, stirring occasionally. Remove the pan from the heat, then add the medium egg and breadcrumbs and mix well. Season to taste with salt and pepper. Set aside.

❖ On a lightly floured surface, roll the dough out thinly. Using the rim of a wine glass, cut out circles in the dough, re-rolling the dough trimmings, until all the dough is used up.

❖ Place some mushroom farce in the centre of each circle and fold each round in half, pressing the edges firmly together to seal. Arrange the pierozki on the prepared baking sheet and bake in the oven for 10–15 minutes or until golden brown and crisp. Serve warm.

For the dough:

225g/8oz plain flour
½ teaspoon salt
140g/5oz butter
1 small egg, beaten or 2 egg yolks
1 tablespoon sour cream

For the mushroom farce (filling):

85g/3oz dried boletus mushrooms,
    soaked in warm water and drained
25g/1oz butter
1 small onion, finely chopped
1 medium egg, beaten
1 tablespoon dried breadcrumbs
salt and freshly ground black pepper

Fried Carp

For many years, carp has been the supreme fish in Polish cooking. It was bred as early as the 13th century and one of the noblest types of this fish, the famous royal carp, was reared in Poland. It is sometimes said that a scale of the royal carp (served on Christmas Eve), hidden in a wallet, brings money.

Serves 4

Preparation time 25 minutes, plus standing time • Cooking time 10 minutes

1 whole carp, about
   900g–1.3kg/2–3lb in weight,
   cleaned and scaled
salt and freshly ground black pepper
plain flour, for sprinkling
1 medium egg, beaten
dry breadcrumbs, for coating
2 tablespoons sunflower oil
25g/1oz butter

❖ Fillet the carp and cut each fillet in half to make a total of 4 portions. Place the fillets on a plate and sprinkle with salt. Set aside to stand for 30 minutes.

❖ Rinse the fish fillets and pat dry with absorbent kitchen paper. Sprinkle a little flour into a shallow dish and season with freshly ground black pepper. Place the beaten egg in another dish and sprinkle the breadcrumbs into a third dish.

❖ Dip each fish fillet into the seasoned flour to coat all over. Shake off any excess. Dip the floured fillets into the beaten egg, draining off any excess. Finally, dip each fillet into the breadcrumbs, making sure they are evenly coated all over.

❖ Heat the oil and butter in a large frying pan until the butter is melted. Add the coated fish fillets and fry over quite a high heat for 2–3 minutes on each side, until cooked, light golden brown and crisp all over.

❖ Lift the fillets out of the pan and drain briefly on absorbent kitchen paper. Serve immediately. In Poland, fried carp is traditionally served with horseradish sauce, cooked cabbage and mushrooms.

Dried Fruit Compote

This dessert can be enjoyed all year round but is especially popular during the festive period. It may be served warm or cold. Dried fruit compote dates back as far as porridge, to pre-Christian times when the fruits were dried in the sun.

Serves 4–6

Preparation time 10 minutes, plus soaking time • Cooking time 10 minutes

450g/1lb mixed dried fruit or prunes
300g/10½oz granulated sugar
finely grated zest and juice of 1 lemon
1 cinnamon stick
6 whole cloves
2 tablespoons brandy (optional)

❖ Rinse the dried fruit in cold water, then place the fruit in a bowl, pour over 450ml/16fl oz cold water and leave to soak for several hours or overnight.

❖ Strain the fruit, reserving the fruit and soaking juices separately. Place the juices in a pan, add the sugar and heat gently, stirring continuously, until the sugar has dissolved.

❖ Pour this mixture over the fruit, add the lemon zest and juice, cinnamon stick, cloves and brandy, if using and stir to mix. Set aside to cool, then refrigerate before serving. Discard the cinnamon and cloves before serving.

Casserole of Venison

This warming dish brightens the darkest winter days in northern Scotland!

Serves 4   *Preparation time 30 minutes • Cooking time 2 hours*

❖   Preheat the oven to 170°C/325°F/Gas Mark 3. Heat the oil in a heavy-based, ovenproof casserole dish, add the venison pieces and cook until browned all over, stirring frequently. Remove the venison pieces from the pan using a slotted spoon and set aside. Add the onions and mushrooms to the juices and cook for 5 minutes, stirring occasionally.

❖   Add the stock to the pan, stirring to loosen the juices and residues in the pan. Return the venison to the pan and add the wine, bramble jelly, sultanas and bouquet garni. Bring to the boil, stirring, then cover and cook in the oven for about 2 hours, or until the venison is cooked and tender, stirring once or twice during cooking.

❖   Meanwhile, place the potatoes in a greased, ovenproof dish in layers with the cream, dots of butter and seasoning, ending with a few dots of butter. Bake in the oven for the last 45–60 minutes of the venison cooking time, until golden brown and bubbling.

For the venison casserole:

450g/1lb venison haunch or shoulder
    meat, cut into 2.5cm/1in cubes and
    coated in seasoned flour
salt and freshly ground black pepper
2 tablespoons sunflower oil
1 red onion, finely chopped
55g/2oz fresh wild mushrooms, sliced
600ml/1 pint vegetable or beef stock
300ml/½ pint red wine
2 tablespoons bramble jelly
25g/1oz sultanas
1 bouquet garni

For the dauphinoise potatoes:

450g/1lb potatoes, par-boiled and
    thinly sliced
300ml/½ pint single cream
85g/3oz butter

Boudins Blancs de Paris

This recipe is taken from Jane Grigson's Charcuterie and French Pork Cookery *(Michael Joseph/Penguin). Ask your butcher for sausage casings.*

❖   The meat and fat must be very finely minced. Put them through the finest mincer blade twice, seasoning with salt, pepper and the spices and adding the onions for the second mincing. Or process with the steel blade, adding the seasonings and onions, then the soaked breadcrumbs and the eggs. If not using a food processor, beat in the eggs and breadcrumbs as thoroughly as possible. Fill the skins slackly.

❖   For their first cooking, in a fish kettle or large saucepan simmer the milk plus 1.2 litres/2 pints water. Lower the sausages gently into the liquid in the poaching tray, or use a metal basket. As the sausages rise to the surface, prick them gently to keep them from exploding; they need about 20 minutes total simmering, and the liquid must never boil.

❖   Raise the sausages gently out of the poaching liquid and leave them to drain. The next day they are ready to eat and can be grilled, brushed with melted butter, or fried.

250g/8oz roast chicken or uncooked
    breast
250g/8oz lean pork such as loin
500g/1¼lb hard back fat mixed with
    flare fat from around the kidney
350g/12oz chopped onion
50g/2oz breadcrumbs soaked in 4–6
    tablespoons hot milk or light cream
3 eggs
1 level tablespoon salt
1 teaspoon white pepper
1 teaspoon quatre-épices or ground
    allspice

For the poaching:

600ml/1 pint milk

Fondue

The history of fondue is an epic. It is astonishing to find a recipe in Homer's Iliad. *Surely the mixture of Pramnos wine, grated goat's cheese and white flour he described was a fondue? The heritage of what is usually considered the Swiss national dish is restored to Switzerland by Jean-Anthelme Brillat-Savarin in his book* Physiologie du Goût, *but it seems that the fondue he ate had tenuous links with the dish we enjoy so much today. 'This fondue originated in Switzerland. It is nothing but scrambled eggs with cheese in certain proportions which time and experience have developed!' The following recipe, however, is both delicious and quite authentic, the legacy of many generations.*

Serves 4   *Preparation time 15 minutes • Cooking time 10–15 minutes*

❖   Rub the inside of an earthenware fondue pot with the garlic. Discard the garlic. Pour the wine into the fondue pot, then heat gently until almost boiling.

❖   Add the gruyere and emmental cheeses, and continue heating, stirring continuously. In a small bowl, blend the cornflour with the kirsch. When the cheese mixture is almost boiling, stir in the blended cornflour mixture. Season to taste with black pepper and nutmeg. A fondue must be creamy – not too thick but sufficient to coat the bread well.

❖   Transfer the fondue pot to a fondue burner. Serve the bread separately. Using a fork, dip the bread into the cheese fondue and remember to stir the fondue with each piece of bread. The fondue should be kept at simmering point whilst eating.

❖   Use Raclette cheese from Valais in place of the gruyere and emmental cheeses. Plum brandy is also sometimes used instead of kirsch.

1 clove garlic
300–400ml/10–14fl oz dry white
    wine
350g/12oz gruyere cheese, grated
350g/12oz emmental cheese, grated
15g/½oz cornflour
2 tablespoons kirsch
freshly ground black pepper and
    freshly grated nutmeg, to season
600g/1lb 5oz bread, cut into 4cm/
    1½in cubes

Swede Casserole (Lanttulaatikko)

Casserole dishes are a major part of the hot food served at Christmas in Finland. They are very useful from the cook's point of view because they can be prepared well in advance and will keep for 2–3 days in a cool place. Homemade vegetable casseroles are Finnish cuisine at its best: nutritious, easy to prepare and exceptionally economical.

Serves 4   *Preparation time 30 minutes • Cooking time 1 hour*

❖   Preheat the oven to 170'°C/325°F/Gas Mark 3. Cook the potatoes and swedes in a saucepan of lightly salted, boiling water for 10–15 minutes, or until tender. Drain, then mash the potatoes and swedes and place in a bowl.

❖   Add the syrup, egg, ground spices, 1 tablespoon butter and the seasoning to the mashed vegetables and mix well.

❖   Transfer the mixture to an ovenproof dish and sprinkle the remaining breadcrumbs over the top. Dot the butter over the surface.

❖   Bake in the oven for about 1 hour, until golden brown. Serve with cooked fresh green vegetables such as spinach and French beans.

4 potatoes, diced (approx. 1 kg/
    2lb 4 oz)
2 medium-sized swedes, diced
    (approx. 1 kg/2lb 4oz)
salt and ground white pepper
3 tablespoons dark or golden syrup
1 medium egg, beaten
½ teaspoon ground nutmeg
½ teaspoon ground ginger
4 tablespoons butter
40g/1½oz fresh breadcrumbs

Christmas Pudding

Start making this traditional English pudding a month before Christmas, involving all the family in the stirring. Use a wooden spoon – traditionally in memory of Christ's crib – and give everyone a turn. They should stir with eyes firmly shut and make a wish at the same time. This recipe is taken from Henrietta Green's Festive Food of England.

Makes 5 x 450g/1lb puddings

Preparation time: 1 hour • Cooking time: 6 hours in advance, then 2–3 hours on the day

❖ Mix together the chopped fruit and nuts and the orange and lemon zest and juices. Sift the flour into a bowl and add the breadcrumbs, suet, sugar and spices. Add the mixed fruits to the bowl and mix thoroughly. Whisk the eggs with the stout and rum. Pour into the mixture and stir thoroughly until all the ingredients are well blended. This is hard work and could take at least half an hour.

❖ Spoon the mixture into greased pudding basins – you will need 5 x 450g/1lb or an equivalent combination – filling them to within 2.5cm/1in of the rim. Cover first with a layer of greaseproof paper and then with a layer of pleated foil, to allow the pudding to rise during cooking. Tie securely with string. Steam the puddings for at least 6 hours; do not forget to top up the pan with boiling water. Remove and store in a cool dry place.

❖ On the day, steam the pudding for a further 2–3 hours. Then turn it out and drench it in heated rum. Set it alight and bring to the table, where it should be greeted with plenty of oohs and ahhhs of anticipation.

225g/8oz prunes, stoned and chopped
225g/8oz raisins, chopped if desired
225g/8oz currants, chopped if desired
225g/8oz sultanas, chopped if desired
225g/8oz chopped mixed candied peel
115g/4oz grated cooking apple
115g/4oz chopped blanched almonds
grated zest and juice of 1 orange
grated zest and juice of 1 lemon
225g/8oz self-raising flour
225g/8oz breadcrumbs
225g/8oz shredded suet
225g/8oz soft brown sugar
5ml/1 teaspoon mixed spice
5ml/1 teaspoon cinnamon
5ml/1 teaspoon grated nutmeg
5ml/1 teaspoon ground ginger
3 eggs, beaten
300ml/½pint stout
70ml/4 tablespoons rum
extra rum for serving

Crêpes St Sylvestre

The feast of St Sylvestre falls on December 31st, New Year's Eve, and in Belgium this is a traditional dish eaten to celebrate the occasion.

Serves 6-8

Preparation time 20 minutes, plus soaking time • Cooking time 25-30 minutes

❖ Place the candied peel and raisins in a bowl, pour over the 100ml/3½fl oz rum and stir to mix. Set aside for at least 1 hour.

❖ Place the milk, flour, salt, caster sugar, butter, egg yolks and cinnamon in a bowl and beat together until smooth. Add the soaked fruit and rum and mix well. In a separate bowl, whisk the egg whites until stiff, then fold them into the fruit mixture.

❖ Heat a little oil in an 18cm/7in heavy-based frying pan until hot, then pour off any surplus. Pour or spoon in just enough fruit batter to thinly coat the base of the pan. Cook for 1–2 minutes, until golden brown, then turn and cook the second side until golden.

❖ Place the cooked crepe on a plate and keep hot. Repeat with the remaining fruit batter to make about 16 crepes, piling the cooked crepes on top of each other with greaseproof paper in between each one.

❖ To serve, spread each crepe with a small spoonful of jam and fold each one into four. Sprinkle with sifted icing sugar, place on a large serving plate and keep warm. Pour a healthy portion of rum over the crepes, set alight and serve immediately. Serve with a dollop of fresh cream or creme fraiche.

100g/3½oz mixed candied peel
25g/1oz raisins
100ml/3½fl oz rum, plus extra for
  serving
500ml/18fl oz milk
150g/5½oz plain flour, sifted
pinch of salt
25g/1oz caster sugar
25g/1oz butter, softened
3 medium eggs, separated
pinch of ground cinnamon
sunflower oil, for frying

apricot jam, for spreading
sifted icing sugar, to serve

Chestnut Dome

For many Europeans, staying at the Ritz Hotel in London is a tradition – or an ambition! With thanks to Chef, here is a Ritz recipe for a special Christmas sweet.

Serves 8–10

Preparation time 1 hour, plus cooling and chilling time • Cooking time 4 minutes

❖ Brush a large charlotte or similar mould with a little oil and set aside. Preheat the oven to 240°C/475°F/Gas Mark 9. Lightly grease a large baking sheet, line with greaseproof paper, grease the paper and set aside. Make the sponge cake. In a bowl, whisk 4 whole eggs with 175g/6oz caster sugar until thick, pale and creamy. Fold in the ground almonds and set aside.

❖ In a separate bowl, whisk the remaining whole egg until pale and creamy, then fold in the flour and set aside. In another bowl, whisk the egg whites and icing sugar together until stiff. Fold the whisked egg white and flour mixtures into the ground almond mixture, mixing well.

❖ Spread the mixture thinly over the prepared baking sheet and bake in the oven for about 4 minutes, or until cooked and golden. Dust with caster sugar, then turn onto a wire rack. Carefully peel off the paper and leave the sponge cake to cool, then cut into fingers, soak in some coffee liqueur or dissolved coffee and use to line the prepared mould. Set aside.

❖ Make the bavarois filling. Heat the milk in a heavy-based saucepan until almost boiling, then remove from the heat and set aside. In a bowl, whisk the egg yolks and sugar together until thick and creamy. Gradually whisk in the hot milk, then strain back into the pan.

❖ Cook over a low heat, stirring continuously, until the mixture thickens enough to lightly coat the back of a wooden spoon – do not allow the mixture to boil or it will curdle. Remove from the heat, pour into a chilled bowl, cover with a piece of dampened greaseproof paper (this prevents a skin forming) and set aside to cool.

❖ Sprinkle the gelatine over 4 tablespoons water in a small bowl and leave to soak for a few minutes. Place the bowl over a pan of simmering water and stir until dissolved. Cool slightly. Stir the gelatine, chestnut puree, chopped chestnuts and whipped double cream into the cooled custard, mixing well. Pour into the sponge-lined mould, then cover and refrigerate for several hours or overnight, until set. To serve, carefully turn out onto a serving plate and decorate with piped rosettes of whipped cream and whole glazed chestnuts.

For the sponge:

vegetable oil, for greasing
5 medium eggs
175g/6oz caster sugar, plus extra
    for dusting
175g/6oz ground almonds
200g/7oz plain flour, sifted
6 medium egg whites
25g/1oz icing sugar, sifted

coffee liqueur or instant coffee
    dissolved in a little warm water,
    for soaking

For the bavarois filling:

600ml/1 pint milk
3 medium egg yolks
25g/1oz caster sugar
1 sachet powdered gelatine
150g/5½oz sweet chestnut puree
55g/2oz sweet chestnuts, finely
    chopped
300ml/½ pint double cream,
    whipped

whipped cream and whole glazed
    chestnuts, to decorate

Chestnut Parfait

Although it may not appear so from the list of ingredients, this French dessert is actually very light. It is certainly very delicious!

Serves 6–8   *Preparation time 25 minutes, plus chilling time*

❖ Brush a 2 litre (3½ pint) charlotte mould with a little oil and set aside. Pour the rum or maraschino into a small bowl and sprinkle the gelatine over the top. Leave to soak for a few minutes, then place the bowl over a pan of simmering water and stir until dissolved. Set aside.

❖ Place the chestnut purée in a bowl and mash or beat until smooth. In a separate bowl, whip the cream with the sugar and vanilla essence to form soft peaks, then fold half into the chestnut purée. Cover and place the remaining cream in the fridge.

vegetable oil, for greasing
125ml/4fl oz dark rum or
   maraschino
1 sachet powdered gelatine
two 400g/14oz cans chestnut purée
600ml/1 pint double cream
140g/5oz caster sugar
¼ teaspoon vanilla essence
140g/5oz marrons glacés or candied
   chestnuts, chopped

5–7 marrons glacés or crystallised
   violets, to decorate

❖ Fold the gelatine into the chestnut purée mixture, mixing well. Fold in the chopped marrons glacés. Turn the mixture into the prepared charlotte mould and level the surface. Chill for 6–8 hours or overnight, until firm and set.

❖ Carefully unmould the dessert onto a serving plate. Fill a piping bag with the remaining cream and pipe lines or swirls of cream down the sides of the dessert at equal intervals, to decorate. Pipe a large rosette or spiral swirl on top. Decorate with marrons glaces or crystallised violets and serve immediately.

Christmas Log (La Bûche de Noël)

The Yule log is one of the oldest of Christmas traditions (see page 51). This luscious chocolate version, from France, originally recalled ancient times when the log represented warmth in the depths of winter and the promise of spring to come.

Serves 6–8   *Preparation time 35 minutes • Cooking time 8–10 minutes*

❖ Preheat the oven to 200°C/400°F/Gas Mark 6. Place a large sheet of greaseproof paper on a baking sheet and set aside. Make the sponge. Put the sugar, whole eggs and egg yolk in a bowl, place over a pan of hot water and whisk until thick, pale and creamy. Remove from the heat and whisk until cool.

❖ Sift half the flour over the egg mixture and fold in lightly with a metal spoon. Fold in half the melted butter, then fold in the remaining sifted flour and then the remaining melted butter.

140

❖ Spread the mixture over the greaseproof paper on the baking sheet, to form a rectangle about 1½cm/⅝in thick. Bake in the oven for 8–10 minutes, until golden brown, risen and firm to the touch.

❖ Meanwhile, place a sheet of greaseproof paper over a damp teatowel. Turn the cooked sponge onto the paper, trim off the crusty edges and roll up the cake with the paper inside. Place seamside down on a wire rack and leave to cool.

❖ Make the icing. Place the sugar, chocolate and 1 teaspoon water in a bowl and place the bowl over a pan of simmering water. Stir until melted and a thick paste is formed, then remove the bowl from the pan. Whisk in the egg yolks, then gradually beat in the melted butter until thoroughly mixed.

❖ Unroll the sponge cake and remove the paper, then spread one-third of the chocolate icing over the sponge and re-roll. Place on a serving plate and spread the remaining chocolate icing all over the sponge roll, covering it completely. Mark lines with a fork to resemble tree bark, then chill for 1 hour before serving. Dust with sifted icing sugar just before serving. Serve in slices.

For the sponge:

75g/2¾oz caster sugar
3 medium eggs, plus 1 medium egg
    yolk
75g/2¾oz plain flour
25g/1oz butter, melted

For the icing:

125g/4½oz caster sugar
50g/1¾oz plain chocolate, broken into
    squares
5 medium egg yolks
250g/9oz butter, melted

sifted icing sugar, to decorate

Mixed Fruit Soup

This is a warming dessert enjoyed in Finland during the cold winter months.

Serves 4

Preparation time 5 minutes, plus overnight soaking time

Cooking time 15–20 minutes

❖ Rinse the dried fruit in cold water, then place in a large bowl with 100g/3½oz of the sugar, cover with 2 litres/3½ pints cold water and stir to mix. Leave to soak overnight.

❖ Transfer the soaked fruit and liquid to a pan and add the cinnamon stick and salt, if using. Cover bring to the boil, then reduce the heat and simmer until the fruit is soft, stirring occasionally. Remove the fruit from the cooking juices using a slotted spoon and place the fruit in a serving dish. Remove and discard the cinnamon stick.

❖ Mix the cornflour or potato flour with a little water and stir into the cooking juices. Heat gently, stirring continuously, until the liquid comes to the boil and thickens. Simmer for 3 minutes, stirring. Pour the thickened cooking juices over the fruit and sprinkle the remaining sugar over the top. Ladle into bowls and serve.

450g/1lb mixed dried fruit, chopped if
    large pieces of fruit
150g/5½oz caster sugar
1 cinnamon stick
pinch of salt (optional)
3 tablespoons cornflour or potato flour

Cranberry Pudding
(Spanguoliu Kisielius)

The lightness of this Lithuanian dessert makes it a welcome conclusion to a rich meal! Its stunning deep garnet colour makes it even more appealing.

Serves 4–6

Preparation time 15 minutes, plus cooling and chilling time
Cooking time 20–25 minutes

❖ Place the cranberries in a pan and add 1.7 litres/3 pints warm water. Cover and bring to a gentle boil – by this stage the cranberries should have begun to burst.

❖ Remove from the heat and strain the cranberries, reserving the fruit and cooking juices separately. Place the cranberries in a blender or food processor and blend until smooth, then mix the cranberry purée and reserved cooking juices together.

❖ Measure this mixture to determine how much cornflour is needed to thicken the mixture enough to make the pudding set sufficiently – for each 225ml/8fl oz fruit mixture, use 1 teaspoon cornflour. Dissolve the appropriate amount of cornflour in a little of the fruit mixture and set aside.

❖ Place the remaining fruit mixture in a pan and add sugar to taste - for a medium sweet pudding, add 100g/3½oz for each 450ml/16fl oz fruit mixture. Add the cinnamon sticks and cloves and bring to a gentle boil, then remove and discard the cinnamon and cloves.

❖ Stir in the blended cornflour mixture and continue to heat gently, stirring continuously, until the mixture thickens – the cornflour mixture will change from a cloudy solution to a clear, deep garnet colour. As soon as the mixture has thickened and become clear, remove from the heat and pour into 1 large or several individual serving dishes. Set aside to cool. Serve cold or chill before serving.

450g/1lb fresh cranberries
cornflour, to thicken
granulated sugar, to taste
3 cinnamon sticks
5 whole cloves

Sweet Scrambled Eggs

This is a typical example of a much-loved dessert from the Minho province of Portugal.

Serves 4

Preparation time 5 minutes, plus cooling time • Cooking time 20 minutes

❖ Place the sugar in a pan with 125ml/4fl oz water and heat gently, stirring, until the sugar has dissolved. Add the ground almonds and breadcrumbs and cook for a couple of minutes, stirring.

❖ Add the raisins, butter, port, salt and cinnamon stick and gently bring to the boil. Simmer for 2–3 minutes, stirring. Add the egg yolks and heat gently, stirring continuously and vigorously, until the mixture just comes to the boil.

❖ Pour into a serving dish and allow to cool before serving. This dessert will thicken as it cools. Refrigerate before serving, if liked, and discard the cinnamon stick before serving.

150g/5½oz granulated sugar
4 tablespoons ground almonds
2 thin slices bread (crusts removed),
    made into breadcrumbs
1 tablespoon raisins
1 tablespoon butter
2 tablespoons port
pinch of salt
1 cinnamon stick
6 medium egg yolks, well-beaten

Delia Smith's Classic Christmas Cake

This, with no apologies, is a Christmas cake that has been in print for 21 years, has been made and loved by thousands and is, along with the Traditional Christmas Pudding, one of the most popular recipes Delia Smith has produced. It's rich, dark and quite moist, so will not suit those who like a crumblier texture.

This recipe is © Delia Smith 1990 and is reproduced by permission from Delia Smith's Christmas *(published by BBC Books)*

Makes one 20cm/8in round or one 18cm/7in square cake

Preparation time 50 minutes, plus 12 hours standing time

Cooking time 4½–4¾ hours

❖ You will need a deep 20cm/8in round cake tin or a deep 18cm/7in square tin, greased and lined with greaseproof paper. Tie a band of brown paper round the outside of the tin for extra protection. Set aside.

❖ You need to begin this cake the night before you want to bake it. All you do is weigh out the dried fruit and mixed peel, place it in a mixing bowl and mix in the brandy as evenly and thoroughly as possible. Cover the bowl with a clean tea-cloth and leave the fruit aside to absorb the brandy for 12 hours.

❖ Next day, preheat the oven to 140°C/275°F/Gas Mark 1. Then measure out all the rest of the ingredients, ticking them off to make sure they're all there. The treacle will be easier to measure if you remove the lid and place the tin in a small pan of barely simmering water.

❖ Now begin the cake by sifting the flour, salt and spices into a large mixing bowl, lifting the sieve up high to give the flour a good airing. Next, in a separate large mixing bowl, whisk the butter and sugar together until it's light, pale and fluffy.

❖ Now beat the eggs in a separate bowl and add them to the creamed mixture a tablespoonful at a time; keep the whisk running until all the egg is incorporated. If you add the eggs slowly by degrees like this the mixture won't curdle. If it does, don't worry, any cake full of such beautiful things can't fail to taste good!

❖ When all the egg has been added fold in the flour and spices, using gentle, folding movements and not beating at all (this is to keep all that precious air in). Now fold in the fruit, peel, chopped nuts and treacle and finally the grated lemon and orange zests.

450g/1lb currants
175g/6oz sultanas
175g/6oz raisins
55g/2oz glace cherries, rinsed, dried and finely chopped
55g/2oz mixed candied peel, finely chopped
3 tablespoons brandy
225g/8oz plain flour
½ teaspoon salt
¼ teaspoon freshly grated nutmeg
½ teaspoon ground mixed spice
225g/8oz unsalted butter
225g/8oz soft brown sugar
4 large eggs
55g/2oz almonds, chopped (the skins can be left on)
1 dessertspoon black treacle
finely grated zest of 1 lemon
finely grated zest of 1 orange
115g/4oz whole blanched almonds (only if you don't intend to ice the cake)

❖   Next, using a large kitchen spoon, transfer the cake mixture into the prepared tin, spread it out evenly with the back of a spoon and, if you don't intend to ice the cake, lightly drop the whole blanched almonds in circles all over the surface.

❖   Finally, cover the top of the cake with a double square of greaseproof paper with a 50p-size hole in the centre (this gives extra protection during the long, slow cooking). Bake the cake on the lowest shelf of the oven for 4½–4¾ hours. Sometimes it can take up to ½–¾ hour longer than this, but in any case don't look till at least 4 hours have passed.

❖   Cool the cake for 30 minutes in the tin, then remove it to a wire rack to finish cooling. When it's cold, 'feed' it with brandy (make a few holes in the top and bottom of the cake with a thin darning needle and spoon over a few teaspoonfuls of brandy to soak in through the holes and permeate the cake), wrap it in double greaseproof paper secured with an elastic band and either wrap again in foil or store in an airtight tin. You can now feed it at odd intervals until you need to ice or eat it.

Delia Smith's Icing for a Ribboned Parcel Cake

This recipe is © Delia Smith 1990 and is reproduced by permission from Delia Smith's Christmas *(published by BBC Books)*

❖ First sift the icing sugar into a large bowl, then add 1½ egg whites, which is just under 2 fl oz/55ml, and reserve the rest of the egg white for later. Add the liquid glucose. Now start to mix everything with a wooden spoon and then finish off with your hands.

❖ As soon as you have a ball of icing, transfer it to a surface dusted with icing sugar and start to knead it in the same way as you would knead bread dough. (I'm afraid it will take 10 minutes or so, so you may need some good music on – or else use it as an opportunity to get rid of all your hidden aggressions!)

❖ If the dough becomes a bit sticky just add a little more sifted icing sugar. When the 10 minutes are up, leave the icing on one side covered with a cloth for 30 minutes.

1¼lb/560g icing sugar, plus extra for dusting
2 egg whites, size 1
3 level tablespoons liquid glucose (available from chemists)

❖ Roll out all the icing to cover the cake completely (without leaving any aside for trimmings). Then take 2 metres/2 yards of any ribbon of your choice; red, green, silver or gold. In the photograph we used some silver metallic strips that have had sequins stamped out of them. These are available from dressmakers who specialise in weddings, and sometimes from florists.

❖ First measure the lengths needed to make the parcel effect and fix these firmly, using large dressmaking pins with little bobbles on the ends. Then make the rest of the ribbon into a large bow and affix this in the same way.

❖ Store the cake in a large container till needed. Before serving be careful to remove the pins securing the ribbon.

Wartime Christmas Cake

Christmas or birthday celebration meals could be dreary affairs on wartime rations in Britain; therefore people tended to store food and bring it out to liven up special occasions. In the summer of 1940 the Ministry of Food banned the use of icing on wedding cakes in an effort to reduce the demand for sugar. Shops began to hire out cardboard cakes decorated with chalk icing sugar. The real cake, which was much smaller, would be hidden underneath the cardboard cover.

Necessity gave birth to a great deal of invention, as in this recipe where a bicarbonate of soda mixture replaces eggs.

Makes one 18cm/7in cake *Preparation time 25 minutes • Cooking time 3 hours*

❖ Preheat the oven to 220°C/425°F/Gas Mark 7. Grease and line a deep 18cm/7in round cake tin and set aside. Place the carrot and syrup in a small pan and cook over a low heat for a few minutes, stirring. Remove from the heat and set aside.

❖ Cream the sugar and margarine together in a bowl until light and fluffy. Stir the bicarbonate of soda into the carrot and syrup mixture, then beat this into the creamed mixture.

❖ Stir in the dried fruit and essences. Fold in the flour and cinnamon, then add enough warmed milk to make a soft, moist mixture.

❖ Transfer the mixture to the prepared tin, level the surface, then make a deep hole in the centre with a spoon – this stops the centre of the cake from rising too much during cooking. Place in the hot oven, then immediately reduce the oven temperature to 150°C/300°F/Gas Mark 2 and bake for 3 hours.

❖ Turn out and cool on a wire rack. Store wrapped in foil or in an airtight container. Serve in slices.

115g/4oz carrot, finely grated
2 tablespoons golden syrup
85g/3oz caster sugar
115g/4oz margarine
1 teaspoon bicarbonate of soda
175g/6oz mixed dried fruit
½ teaspoon vanilla essence
½ teaspoon almond essence
350g/12oz self-raising flour, sifted
1 teaspoon ground cinnamon
about 175ml/6fl oz warm milk

Luxury Mince Pies

These traditional and very appetising Scottish mince pies are delicious served warm or cold, with sweetened double cream, flavoured with Scotch whisky! Minced meat was originally included in the filling, with spices added to represent the gifts of the Three Wise Men. Mince pies were originally oval, the shape of the manger, and had three slits cut in them, one for each of the Wise Men.

If you want to make your own mincemeat, a recipe is given on page 82.

Makes 12

Preparation time 25 minutes, plus 30 minutes chilling time
Cooking time 15–20 minutes

❖ Preheat the oven to 180°C/350°F/Gas Mark 4. Place the flour, cornflour, icing sugar and butter in a food processor and whizz together to form a firm, smooth dough (alternatively, place the flour, cornflour, icing sugar and butter in a bowl and rub the butter into the dry ingredients, then continue kneading the mixture lightly until it forms a dough). Gather the dough into a ball, then knead lightly, wrap in greaseproof paper and chill for 30 minutes.

❖ Roll out the pastry on a lightly floured surface and cut out 12 rounds with a 7.5cm/3in fluted cutter and 12 smaller rounds with a 5.5cm/2¼in fluted cutter. Line 6cm/2½in patty tins with the larger rounds and fill each one with some mincemeat.

❖ Dampen the edges of the smaller rounds with water and place them firmly on top of the mincemeat. Using a sharp knife, make a small slit in the top of each, if liked. Brush the tops lightly with beaten egg white and sprinkle with flaked almonds. Bake in the oven for 15–20 minutes, until golden brown. Place on a wire rack to cool. Serve warm or cold.

200g/7oz plain flour
100g/3½oz cornflour
100g/3½oz icing sugar
200g/7oz butter
200g/7oz mincemeat

beaten egg white, to glaze
flaked almonds, for sprinkling

Vasilopitta (St Basil's Cake)

This traditional Cypriot cake is baked with a coin hidden inside. It is made especially for New Year's Day and it is cut soon after midnight on New Year's Eve when people are still sitting around the table eating and enjoying themselves. The person who finds the hidden coin is considered to be the lucky one of the year.

According to legend, when the province of Caesarea was being attacked by the Cappadocians, St Basil appealed to his people to help defend their country by offering whatever they could afford. The people responded with gifts of gold rings, bracelets, money, all sorts of valuable objects. By a miracle, the Cappadocians gave up their plans and St Basil, not knowing how to give the contribution back to each individual, made loaves of bread in which he hid the precious objects. He called together everyone who had made a donation and offered each of them a loaf. The people rejoiced to find a precious object in the bread. This cake has been baked ever since to commemorate St Basil's diplomacy.

Serves 12–16   *Preparation time 35 minutes, plus rising time • Cooking time 40 minutes*

❖   Place the star anise in a small pan with 125ml/4fl oz water and bring to the boil. Remove from heat and set it to one side to cool slightly, then strain and reserve the liquid.

❖   Meanwhile, sprinkle the yeast over the warm milk in a bowl and stir to dissolve the yeast. Blend in 55g/2oz flour and stir until smooth. Cover and set aside in a warm place for about 30 minutes until the mixture has risen.

❖   In a bowl, beat the eggs and sugar together until frothy, then add the orange zest and melted butter and beat until well mixed. In a large bowl, mix the remaining flour and salt together and make a well in the middle. Add the aniseed liquid and the yeast and egg mixtures and beat together until the mixture forms a dough.

❖ Knead the dough on a lightly floured surface for about 10 minutes or until smooth and elastic. Place it in an oiled bowl, cover with a clean teatowel and leave to rise in a warm place for 1–2 hours, or until doubled in size.

❖ Grease a baking sheet and set aside. Knead the dough again on a lightly floured surface for 2–3 minutes, then shape the dough into a round and place on the baking sheet. Cover and leave to rise again in a warm place until doubled in size.

❖ Meanwhile, preheat the oven to 190°C/375°F/Gas Mark 5. Lightly brush the dough with beaten egg to glaze and sprinkle with sesame seeds and flaked almonds.

❖ Bake in the oven for about 40 minutes until cooked and golden. Transfer to a wire rack to cool. Once cool, make a deep slit in the side of the cooked cake. Wrap a small coin in a piece of foil and insert the coin into the cake. Dust the top of the cake with sifted icing sugar and serve in slices.

1 teaspoon dried star anise
1 tablespoon dried yeast
125ml/4fl oz lukewarm milk
750g/1lb 10oz strong plain white flour
4 medium eggs
200g/7oz caster sugar
1 teaspoon finely grated orange zest
175g/6oz butter, melted
½ teaspoon salt

beaten egg, to glaze
sesame seeds and flaked almonds, for sprinkling

sifted icing sugar, to decorate

Lebkuchen

As well as being delicious, these traditional Austrian biscuits are ideal for hanging on the Christmas tree as edible decorations. As soon as you take them out of the oven, pierce each one with a skewer, making a hole large enough for a thin ribbon or decorative cord to pass through. Store as instructed below before hanging them on the tree.

Makes 40–50

Preparation time 25 minutes, plus cooling and chilling time • Cooking time 15 minutes

❖ Lightly grease and flour 4 baking sheets. Place the honey in a large pan and heat until it is quite hot but not too hot to touch. Remove pan from the heat, stir in the sugar, ground spices and lemon and orange zests, then set aside to cool.

❖ Stir in the flour, eggs and melted butter. Dissolve the bicarbonate of soda in 1 tablespoon water and add this to the honey mixture. Add the chopped nuts and peel, if using, and work the ingredients together to form a smooth dough. Place in a bowl, cover and leave to rest in a cool place for 12 hours or overnight.

❖ Preheat the oven to 180°C/350°F/Gas Mark 4. Roll out the dough on a lightly floured surface and cut into a variety of shapes using a sharp knife or biscuit cutters. Brush each shape with a little beaten egg white and sprinkle with flaked almonds. Bake in the oven for about 15 minutes or until golden. Place on a wire rack to cool. Store in an airtight container for about 2 weeks before eating.

250g/9oz honey
125g/4½oz caster sugar
3 tablespoons ground cinnamon
1 teaspoon ground allspice
½ teaspoon ground cloves
finely grated zest of ½ lemon
finely grated zest of ½ orange
500g/1lb 2oz plain flour (preferably light rye flour)
2 medium eggs, beaten
85g/3oz butter, melted
1 teaspoon bicarbonate of soda
150g/5½oz mixed finely chopped almonds and candied peel (optional)

beaten egg white, to glaze
flaked almonds, to decorate

Stollen

This popular yeasted cake from Germany is traditionally served to family and friends at Christmas and enjoyed with steaming mugs of hot chocolate or glasses of mulled wine.

Serves 16–20

Preparation time 45 minutes, plus rising time • Cooking time 40-50 minutes

❖ Crumble the yeast into a bowl, then blend in 25g/1oz sugar, 125ml/4fl oz warm milk, 25g/1oz flour and mix well. Cover and leave in a warm place for 15 minutes until frothy.

❖ Place the flour and salt in a large bowl, add the remaining sugar and milk, melted butter, lemon zest, ground spices and the yeast mixture and beat together to mix well. Add the raisins, candied peel and almonds and beat together until the mixture forms a dough.

❖ Knead the dough on a lightly floured surface for about 10 minutes or until smooth and elastic. Place it in an oiled bowl, cover with a clean teatowel and leave to rise in a warm place for about 1 hour, or until doubled in size.

❖ Grease a baking sheet and set aside. Knead the dough again on a lightly floured surface for 2–3 minutes, then roll or shape the dough into a large flat rectangle. Roll the marzipan or almond paste into a long, thin rectangle and place it down the centre of the dough. Fold the dough over the marzipan, overlapping the dough slightly and sealing it down the centre. Seal the ends by pinching them together to enclose the marzipan.

❖ Place, seam-side down, on the prepared baking sheet. Make a few shallow slits across the top with a sharp knife, if liked. Cover and leave to rise again in a warm place for up to an hour, until doubled in size.

❖ Preheat the oven to 200°C/400°F/Gas Mark 6. Bake in the oven for 40–50 minutes until golden brown. Transfer to a wire rack to cool. Dust with sifted icing sugar and serve in slices.

55g/2oz fresh yeast
225g/8oz caster sugar
500ml/18fl oz warm milk
1kg/2lb 4oz strong plain white flour
1 teaspoon salt
225g/8oz butter, melted
finely grated zest of 1 lemon
½ teaspoon ground cardamom
½ teaspoon ground mace
500g/1lb 2oz raisins
115g/4oz candied lemon peel, minced
**   or finely chopped**
115g/4oz candied orange peel, minced
**   or finely chopped**
225g/8oz blanched almonds, minced
**   or finely chopped**
350g/12oz marzipan or almond paste

sifted icing sugar, to serve

Cinnamon Cookies

Since colonial times, when the Spice Islands were an important part of the Dutch Empire, Eastern spices have been a popular feature of Dutch cooking.

Makes about 40   Preparation time 20 minutes • Cooking time 15–20 minutes

❖ Preheat the oven to 180°C/350°F/Gas Mark 4. Grease 3 baking sheets. Cream butter and sugar together in a bowl until light and fluffy. Beat in egg yolks, then fold in flour, salt, cinnamon and enough milk to make a dough, and knead until smooth.

❖ Divide the dough in half and roll out on a lightly floured surface to about 5mm/¼in thick and cut into shapes using biscuit cutters or a sharp knife. Place on the prepared baking sheets and bake in the oven for 15–20 minutes lightly browned.

❖ Transfer to a wire rack to cool. Store in an airtight container.

250g/9oz butter, softened
250g/9oz caster sugar
3 medium egg yolks
500g/1lb 2oz plain flour
½ teaspoon salt
3 teaspoons ground cinnamon
a little milk, to mix

Poppy Seed Rolls (Beigli)

This is a special kind of Christmas 'cake', which comprises rolled pastry filled with a poppy seed or walnut mixture. Beigli are considered an essential part of a Hungarian Christmas.

Makes 4   *Preparation time 30 minutes, plus rising time • Cooking time 30 minutes*

❖   Mix the flour and yeast in a bowl, then rub in the butter. Stir in the icing sugar, then stir in the egg and sour cream to form a firm dough. Knead on a lightly floured surface for about 10 minutes, until smooth, then place in a clean bowl, cover with a clean teatowel and leave to rest in a cool place for 1 hour.

❖   Mix the poppy seeds and sugar with enough milk to make a paste. Cover and set aside.

❖   Grease 2 baking sheets and set aside. Divide the pastry into four equal portions and roll out each portion to form a rectangle. Spread some poppy seed mixture over each rectangle. Roll up each rectangle of dough to enclose the filling, then place the rolls of dough on the prepared baking sheets, cover and leave in a warm place until risen.

❖   Preheat the oven to 190°C/375°F/Gas Mark 5. Brush each dough roll with a little beaten egg or honey to glaze. Bake in the oven for about 30 minutes, until golden brown. Transfer to a wire rack to cool. Dust with sifted icing sugar before serving and serve in slices.

For the pastry:

500g/1lb 2oz strong plain white flour
1 sachet fast-action dried yeast
150g/5½oz butter
100g/3½oz icing sugar, sifted
1 medium egg, beaten
200ml/7fl oz sour cream

For the poppy seed filling:

150g/5½oz poppy seeds
100g/3½oz caster sugar
a little milk, to mix

beaten egg or clear honey, to glaze
sifted icing sugar, to decorate
    (optional)

Cook's Tip

For a change, use a walnut filling in place of the poppy seeds. Mix together 150g/5½oz ground walnuts with 100g/3½oz caster sugar. Add a little milk and mix to form a paste. Use as above in place of the poppy seed filling.

Fried Crullers (Kleinur)

These deep-fried sweet treats originate in Iceland and are best eaten when freshly made.

Serves 6   *Preparation time 25 minutes • Cooking time 15–20 minutes*

❖   Mix the flour, baking powder, cardamom and salt together in a bowl. Add the margarine, sugar, egg and milk and mix thoroughly to form a dough, adding a little extra milk if necessary. On a lightly floured surface, roll the dough out to about 3mm/⅛in thick. Cut the dough diagonally into strips about 2cm/¾in wide and about 10cm/4in long. Make a slit in the centre of each strip and pull one end of each strip through the slit to make a 'cruller'.

❖   Heat the oil in a deep-fryer to 190°C/375°F. Lower the crullers, one at a time, into the hot fat and fry in batches for 3–4 minutes or until cooked and golden brown. Remove and drain on kitchen paper. Keep hot while frying the remaining crullers. Serve hot or cold.

600g/1lb 5oz plain flour
1 tablespoon baking powder
2 teaspoons ground cardamom
1 teaspoon salt
115g/4oz soft margarine
4½ tablespoons caster sugar
1 medium egg, beaten
150ml/¼ pint milk
vegetable oil, for deep-frying

Honey Rings

This is a delicious sweetmeat from Malta.

Makes 20–30

Preparation time 30 minutes, plus cooling time • Cooking time 15–20 minutes

❖ Make the filling. Place the honey or treacle, sugar, tangerine or orange juice, cocoa powder, spice, bicarbonate of soda and anisette into a heavy-based saucepan, add 450ml/16fl oz water and stir to mix. Bring to the boil, then gradually add the semolina, stirring continuously. Simmer until the mixture thickens, stirring, then remove from the heat and set aside to cool.

❖ Meanwhile make the pastry. Place the flour, butter, lard and sugar in a bowl and lightly rub the ingredients together to form breadcrumbs. Add enough cold water, mixing to make a firm, smooth dough. Wrap in greaseproof paper and chill in the refrigerator for at least 30 minutes, before using.

❖ Preheat the oven to 200°C/400°F/Gas Mark 6. Lightly flour 3 baking sheets and set aside. To make the honey rings, roll the pastry out on a lightly floured surface, then cut into long strips about 5cm/2in in width. Place some honey filling along the centre of each pastry strip and roll up the pastry to enclose the filling and form a long roll. Cut the filled pastry rolls into shorter lengths and form each one into a ring, sealing the two ends of each ring together. Cut slits at intervals on top of each ring.

❖ Place the honey rings on the prepared baking sheets and bake in the oven for 15–20 minutes until golden brown. Transfer to a wire rack to cool, then serve.

For the pastry:

700g/1lb 9oz plain flour
115g/4oz butter
115g/4oz lard
115g/4oz caster sugar

For the filling:

700g/1lb 9oz honey or treacle
400g/14oz granulated sugar
juice of 2 tangerines or 1 orange
4 teaspoons cocoa powder, sifted
2 teaspoons ground mixed spice
1 teaspoon bicarbonate of soda
2 tablespoons anisette liqueur
115g/4oz semolina

155

SLOVENIAN BAKING

The baking of Christmas bread is one of the oldest features of the Christmas celebration in Slovenia. In fact, its origins can be traced to pre-Christian times and are a symbol of respect for ancestors, which was particularly important at this season. Christianity, of course, gave bread – and other elements on the Christmas table – an additional symbolic meaning.

Christmas bread has different names in different parts of Slovenia, but the most widespread is *poprtnik* or *poprtnjak*, indicating where it was placed: under a tablecloth (*prt*), on the table or just under the table. In some areas it was the custom to place field tools under or beside the table, and to put a few sheaves of wheat and a pitcher of wine beside the bread. Frequently there were three loaves of special bread, each made from a different flour.

Dried Fruit Bread (Sadni kruh)

This is at its best if it is made a day in advance.

Makes one or two loaves

Preparation time 35 minutes, plus soaking and rising time • Cooking time 1 hour

❖ Make the filling. Place the mixed dried fruit, raisins, sugar, nuts and rum or whisky in a bowl and stir to mix. Set aside and allow the fruit and nuts to soak for at least 2 hours.

❖ Meanwhile, make the dough. Place the flour, yeast, salt and sugar in a large bowl and stir to mix. Add the warm water, butter and eggs and enough warm milk, mixing to make a soft dough.

❖ Turn out onto a floured surface and knead for about 10 minutes or until smooth and elastic. Shape into a ball, place in an oiled bowl, cover with a clean teatowel and leave to rise in a warm place until doubled in size.

❖ Grease a baking sheet and set aside. Knead the dough again on a lightly floured surface for 1–2 minutes, then knead the fruit and nut filling mixture into the dough until thoroughly mixed.

❖ Shape the dough into 1 large round loaf or divide the dough in half and shape into 2 smaller rounds. Place on the prepared baking sheet. Cover and leave to rise in a warm place until doubled in size.

❖ Meanwhile, preheat the oven to 170°C/ 325°F/Gas Mark 3. Lightly brush the top of the loaf(s) with milk to glaze and bake in the oven for 1 hour until risen and golden brown. Transfer to a wire rack to cool. Store in an airtight container and serve the next day, cut into slices.

For the dough:

900g/2lb strong plain white flour
2 sachets fast-action dried yeast
1 tablespoon salt
5 tablespoons caster sugar
75ml/2½fl oz warm water
1 tablespoon butter, melted
2 medium eggs, beaten
225–350ml/8–12fl oz warm milk

For the fruit filling:

450g/1lb mixed dried fruit, chopped
85g/3oz raisins
100g/3½oz caster sugar
150g/5½oz chopped mixed nuts
125ml/4fl oz rum or whisky

milk, for glazing

Variation

Use pineapple, orange or apple juice in place of the rum or whisky.

Exotic Rich Potica

This is a variation on a familiar dish, now usually served as a dessert. It is rendered 'exotic' by the addition of milk to the dough and sour cream to the filling.

Makes 3 loaves *Preparation time 1 hour, plus rising time • Cooking time 1 hour*

❖ Lightly grease three 30cm/12in loaf tins and set aside. Make the yeast starter. Place the yeast, sugar and flour in a bowl and blend in the warm milk. Set aside in a warm place for about 15 minutes until frothy.

❖ Make the dough. Place the milk and butter in a small pan and heat gently until the butter has melted, then remove from the heat and set aside to cool. Place the flour in a large bowl, add the salt, sugar, eggs, egg yolks, cooled milk and butter and yeast mixture and beat thoroughly to form a soft, smooth dough, adding a little extra flour, if necessary.

❖ Turn the dough out onto a lightly floured surface and knead for about 10 minutes until smooth and elastic. Place the dough in an oiled bowl, cover with a clean teatowel and leave to rise in a warm place for 1–2 hours, or until doubled in size.

❖ Meanwhile, make the filling. Heat the double cream and butter in a pan until the butter has melted, then remove from the heat. Place the nuts in a large bowl, pour over the cream mixture, then add the honey, sour cream, sugar, lemon zest and juice, vanilla essence and egg yolks and beat together until well mixed. In a separate bowl, whisk the egg whites until stiff, then fold them into the nut mixture. If the mixture is a little dry, add a little more double cream. Set aside.

❖ Knead the dough again on a lightly floured surface for 2–3 minutes, then divide the dough into 3 equal portions. Roll out one portion of dough on a lightly floured surface to form a rectangle about 5mm/¼in thick. Spread one-third of the walnut filling over the dough, then roll the dough up into a roll. Place in a prepared loaf tin. Repeat with the remaining two portions of dough and filling mixture to make a total of three rolls/loaves. Prick all over the top of the loaves with a fork, then cover with a cloth and leave to rise in a warm place for about 35 minutes.

❖ Meanwhile, preheat the oven to 170°C/325°F/Gas Mark 3. Lightly brush the top of each loaf with melted butter or beaten egg to glaze. Bake in the oven for about 1 hour or until risen and golden brown. Remove from the oven and leave in the tins for about 10 minutes, then turn out and cool on a wire rack. Serve warm or cold in slices.

For the yeast starter:

55g/2oz fresh yeast, crumbled
1 tablespoon caster sugar
1 tablespoon plain flour
125ml/4fl oz warm milk

For the dough:

225ml/8fl oz milk
115g/4oz butter
900g/2lb strong plain white flour
1 teaspoon salt
150g/5½oz caster sugar
2 medium eggs, beaten, plus 4 medium
  egg yolks

For the filling:

225ml/8fl oz double cream
115g/4oz butter
900g/2lb walnuts, ground
175g/6oz honey
225ml/8fl oz sour cream
200g/7oz caster sugar
1 teaspoon finely grated lemon zest
1 teaspoon lemon juice
1 teaspoon vanilla essence
2 medium eggs, separated

melted butter or beaten egg, to glaze

Cook's Tip

If three large loaves are too many for your needs, this recipe works well if you simply halve the quantities, or even divide them by three.

Variation

For the nuts in the filling substitute chocolate or various kinds of fruit. A more savoury filling can be made by omitting the double cream, honey, nuts, peel and vanilla and replacing with 225g/8oz chopped fresh tarragon and 110g/4oz breadcrumbs.

159

Gingerbread Cookies

Gingerbread cookies, together with cardamom bread, are served from St Lucia Day onwards, throughout Christmas in Sweden.

Makes 50   *Preparation time 25 minutes, plus resting time • Cooking time 5–10 minutes*

❖ Place the sugar, treacle or molasses and butter in a saucepan and heat gently until melted, stirring. Pour the mixture into a large bowl and allow to cool a little, then stir in the cream and ground spices. Mix the bicarbonate of soda with a little of the flour and stir into the melted mixture. Add the remaining flour and mix thoroughly to form a smooth dough. Turn out onto a lightly floured surface and knead the dough lightly, then place in a clean bowl, cover and leave to rest overnight.

❖ Preheat the oven to 200°C/400°F/Gas Mark 6. Grease 3 baking sheets and set aside. Roll the dough out on a lightly floured surface to about 5mm/¼in thick and cut into different shapes using biscuit cutters or a sharp knife. Place the shapes on the prepared baking sheets and bake in the oven for 5–10 minutes or until golden. Cool slightly on the baking sheets, then remove and place on a wire rack to cool. Store in an airtight container.

125g/4½oz light soft brown sugar
75ml/2½fl oz black treacle or molasses
100g/3½oz butter
75ml/2½fl oz whipping cream
1½ teaspoons ground ginger
1½ teaspoons ground cinnamon
½ teaspoon ground cloves
1½ teaspoons bicarbonate of soda
350g/12oz plain flour

Glarus Winter Cake

According to a very old recipe, this typical Swiss cake was left outside in the cold for 2 days before it was served. Glarus cake was, therefore, a winter speciality and ideal for serving at Christmas.

Serves 10–12   *Preparation time 20 minutes, plus rising time • Cooking time 50 minutes*

❖ Grease and flour a deep 20cm/8in round cake tin and set aside. Cream the butter and sugar together in a bowl until pale and fluffy. Add the salt, cinnamon, kirsch and eggs and beat thoroughly. Fold in the flour, mixing well. Blend the yeast with the milk in a small bowl, then add this to the creamed mixture. Add the sultanas and 50ml/2fl oz warm water and mix thoroughly. Turn the mixture into the prepared tin, then cover with a clean teatowel and leave to rise in a warm place.

❖ Meanwhile, preheat the oven to 180°C/350°F/Gas Mark 4. Bake the cake for about 50 minutes, until cooked, risen and golden brown. Turn out on to a wire rack and leave to cool. Wrap the cake in foil or greaseproof paper and store in a cool place (not the refrigerator, or the cake will be tough) for 2 days. Serve at room temperature.

200g/7oz butter, softened
200g/7oz caster sugar
pinch of salt
1 teaspoon ground cinnamon
5 teaspoons kirsch
3 medium eggs, beaten
400g/14oz strong white plain flour, sifted
25g/1oz fresh yeast, crumbled
50ml/2fl oz warm milk
150g/5½oz sultanas

Scotch Whisky Liqueur

A deliciously creamy liqueur based on Scotch whisky. Serve well-chilled.

Preparation time 5 minutes, plus chilling time

❖   Place all the ingredients in a bowl and whisk together until thoroughly mixed. Pour the mixture into a bottle(s), seal and store in the refrigerator.

❖   Serve, poured over ice cubes, or, for a delicious dessert, pour over good quality vanilla or chocolate ice cream and enjoy! This liqueur will keep in the refrigerator for up to 4 weeks – if it is given the opportunity!

400g/14oz can condensed milk
400g/14oz can evaporated milk
300ml/½ pint Scotch whisky
1 teaspoon vanilla essence
2 teaspoons coffee granules (dissolved in a little warm water)
1 teaspoon glycerine

Tangerine Liqueur

This fragrant Portuguese liqueur makes an excellent digestif, and can also be used for flavouring cakes, puddings, fruit salads, etc.

Preparation time 15 minutes, plus cooling and standing time

❖   Pour the spirits into a suitable container and add the fruit rind and fruit juice, if using. Cover and leave for 3–4 weeks, to allow the peel to soften, shaking the container occasionally.

❖   Place the sugar in a pan, add 700ml/1¼ pints water and heat gently until the sugar has dissolved, stirring. Bring to the boil and boil rapidly for 3 minutes, then remove the pan from the heat and set aside to cool.

❖   Add the cooled sugar syrup to the spirit mixture and mix well. Leave to stand for 2–3 days.

❖   Filter the liqueur (using a coffee-type filter), then bottle and seal it. Discard the contents of the filter. Store the bottled liqueur in a cool, dark place for several months before serving. The longer you leave it the better. In fact, it should be left to mature for nearly a year.

600ml/1 pint pure spirits (vodka is best as it has a more neutral taste, otherwise use brandy)
pared rind of 6 tangerines or clementines (peeled thinly using a potato peeler)
juice of 3 tangerines or clementines (optional)
700g/1lb 9oz granulated sugar

Cook's Tips

After a couple of months of making the liqueur, taste it for strength and sweetness. If you think it should be stronger, at this stage add a few tablespoons of the spirits (vodka or brandy) used before. In the same way, if you would like it sweeter, make a little more syrup, cool and add to the liqueur. Leave for another few months. The longer you leave it the better. The liqueur will gain in smoothness and aroma, as well as body. It is a good idea to have a liqueur maturing as you use the previous one. They last indefinitely and turn into something really scrumptious as they age.

If using the fruit juice in this recipe, the liqueur will take the name of 'ratafia'. The fruit juice is not strictly necessary for a good result. Note that the rind must be peeled very thinly, avoiding the pith, which is bitter.

Hot Christmas Cordial (Gløgg)

Gløgg is a popular and warming drink served throughout Scandinavia at Christmas. It is difficult to assess how many people this quantity will serve: one Finnish cookery book gives the following as a quantity for 1–6 servings!

Preparation time 15 minutes

❖   Place the red wine, Madeira, if using, sugar, ginger root, cinnamon sticks, cloves, cardamom seeds and orange rind in a saucepan. Heat gently, stirring, until the sugar has dissolved, then continue heating gently until the mixture is very warm, but still a long way from boiling, stirring occasionally.

❖   Mix the raisins and almonds together and place a little of this mixture in the base of small mugs or glasses. Stir the vodka into the hot wine mixture, if using, then strain the mixture into a jug. Discard the contents of the sieve. Pour the steaming liquid into the mugs or glasses, over the fruit and nuts, and serve immediately.

1 bottle (750ml) red wine
2-3 tablespoons Madeira (optional)
100g/3½oz granulated sugar
1 small fresh ginger root, peeled
2 cinnamon sticks
6 whole cloves
½ teaspoon cardamom seeds
thinly pared rind of 1 orange
55g/2oz raisins
25g/1oz blanched, slivered almonds
50ml/2fl oz vodka (optional)

Wassail Cup

The name wassail comes from the Old English for 'be thou whole' and drinking from the wassail bowl was an expression of friendship. At one time, most households in England and Wales kept a bowl of this warming drink ready throughout the Christmas period in case unexpected guests arrived. This recipe is taken from Henrietta Green's Festive Food of England.

Serves 8   *Preparation time: 10 minutes • Cooking time: 30 minutes*

❖   Slit the skin around the centre of the apples and stud them with cloves. Put them in a baking tin with 150ml/¼ pint of the brown ale and bake in a 200°C/400°F/Gas Mark 6 oven for about 30 minutes, basting occasionally.

❖   Heat the remaining brown ale with the sherry, spices and lemon zest and simmer for about 5 minutes. Cut the toast and the baked apples into small pieces and serve the punch very hot, in a punch bowl, with the pieces floating on top.

8 small eating apples
32 cloves
1.5litres/2½pints brown ale
300ml/½pint sweet sherry
pinch of ground cinnamon
pinch of ground ginger
pinch of ground nutmeg
grated zest of 1 lemon
2 slices bread, toasted

A Closing Note

My wonderful 'journeying' around Europe this past year has come to an end – no jet-lag, no baggage problems – my imagination is at home again! It is easy, on returning from holiday, to plunge too quickly and too deeply back into the various problems of day-to-day life; the holiday memories, however enjoyable, have a way of fading all too fast. But for me the memories of this European experience will never fade!

Researching Christmas traditions from Christian country to country has revealed so vividly the incredible influence and reverence that resulted from the birth of that Babe in Bethlehem. We share so many customs, yet each country has its own indelible national stamp. The efforts made to reach home for Christmas, no matter what the distance or difficulties, shone through wherever I looked. This in itself seems to me to form the basis of a great international understanding.

I am part of quite a large family circle, but these past months I feel I have gained a host of not-too-distant continental cousins. I would love to experience a family Christmas in all the European countries mentioned in the book – but, time, I fear will not permit!

From a homely point of view, I shall never again stand by the stove 'on a cold and frosty morning', stirring porridge, without looking back in my mind to the pre- and early Christian days when cereal crops were always at hand, fresh or dried, and this humble, satisfying, cheap food was a prop to life. Known through the ages as patigi, potage or porridge, a revamped, thickened version finally became our revered Christmas pudding. From now on I shall stir the morning porridge with far more respect!

From the initial idea to the moment of completion of this book, there have been contacts far and wide and many stages of search and research over the vast territory of Europe. It is good to remember – although this is a Chinese proverb, not a European one – that 'every journey of a thousand miles begins with a single step'.

With sincere Millennium greetings

STELLA ROSS COLLINS

St Thomas brought Christmas and its message of peace to Finland. The St Thomas's Cross, traditionally whittled from birch, is placed on the table or against a wall as a sign of the saint's protection.

Acknowledgements

The following list represents a very wide range of people and organisations whose contributions have helped to make *Christmas!* a reality. Whether they provided words, illustrations, encouragement or other assistance, the author wishes to express her most grateful thanks.

Sincere appreciation is directed to Embassies, Press, Information & Tourist Offices, Cultural Centres, Institutes and Libraries for showing interest and supplying such helpful material, and to Caroline Taggart, Robert Updegraff and everyone at Kyle Cathie Ltd for their efforts in producing such a handsome book.

My family

Theresa Bartlett

Barbara Brown

Susan Coxon

Peter Crofts

Shirley Edell

Philip Edell

Nicholas Edell

Rosemary Fox

Andrew Ross Collins

Michael Ross Collins

Audrey Stewart

Lord & Lady Stewartby

The National Society for the Prevention of Cruelty to Children

NSPCC Barnet Branch members (co-ordinator Alison Harrow)
The Bridgeman Art Library
The Elisabeth Houtzager Crib Collection
The Fan Museum, London
The Flag Institute Enterprises Ltd
Hamleys, Regent Street, London
Hulton Getty Picture Corporation
The Lindley Library, Royal Horticultural Society
The Meteorological Office
The National Gallery
The Ritz Hotel, London (with particular thanks to the Chef)
Sotheby's Transparency Department
Spink & Son Ltd

HRH, The Duchess of Gloucester
The Rt Hon The Baroness Thatcher of Kesteven, LG, OM, FRS
The Seigneur of Sark, Mr J M Beaumont

Birgitte, Countess of Stockton
Lady Holland-Martin, DBE, DL
Lady Moyra Campbell, CVO
Lady Harris of High Cross
George Evatt, OBE
The Reverend David Lewthwaite
Dr Janez Bogataj, Professor at the Faculty of Arts, University of Ljubljana
Hélène Alexander
Nina Barclay de Tolly
E G Beaton
Elke Bickert
Karya Birchley
G J C Bois
Brita Brooks
Joan M Brown, Head of Home Economics, The Dollar Academy
Ursula Buchan
Annalisa Budtz-Jorgensen
David Burns, Fettes College
Alan Cali
Phyllida Campbell
Sue Collins
Shirley Cleremont
Olive Coghlan
Margaret Cox

Yvonne Cresswell, Manx National Heritage at The Manx Museum
Billie Crook
Marian Crook
Mark Elder
Judit Ferenczi
Marion Forde
Patsy Fostiropoulos
Patrick Gaskell-Taylor
Ann Goddard
Anita Green
Margaret Hammond
Joe Hayes
Pam Hedgecoe
Joke van Heek
Wendy K (Barrie) Henderson, President, St George's OGA
Alessandra Hicks
Sonia Hillsdon
Beatrice Jonker
Eduard S Jonker
Betty King
Loreta & Steven King
Margit Latter
Emma Lile – Assistant Curator, National Museums & Galleries of Wales
Louis McConnell
Judith Mann

Joe Micallef
Cory Mitchell
Daphne Noel
Stephen Oakley
Danielle Pasqualini
George Reynolds
Hilary Roberts
Tatiana Rodionova
Jonas Saladzius
Marcel Sarde
Jacques Schoenmakers
Marcel Schoenmakers
Daniela Scholl
Dorothy Simms
Christine Siracusa
Bryan Smalley
Delia Smith
Pamela Stuart
Nora Taylor
Erja Tikka
Edite Vieira
Judy Waples, Katie & Thomas
Fletcher Watkins
Steve Watt, Tourism Development & Maritime Officer, The Scilly Isles
Paivi Wheeler
Elizabeth Wilson
Penelope Wrong

Index

Publishers' Acknowledgements

The photography on the endpapers, title page and on pp. 53 (right hand column), 54 (styled by Penny Markham), 55, 56, 57, 73, 81, 82, 88, 92, 93, 94–5, 96, 97, 98, 102, 103,104, 105, 106, 111,117, 119, 120, 122, 124, 126–7, 132, 134, 137, 139, 140, 141, 142, 148, 150, 152, 155, 156–7, 158, 160 is by Clay Perry.

The flags on pp. 10–21 are reproduced courtesy of The Flag Institute Enterprises Ltd.

The author and publishers would also like to thank the following for permission to reproduce illustrations: Spink & Son Ltd half-title; The Russian Orthodox Cathedral of the Dormition of the Mother of God and All Saints, Knightsbridge, London SW7 imprint page; GV Press/Studio Markku Alatalo pp. 6–7; Bridgeman Art Library pp. 22–23 (oil on panel c. 1566 by Pieter the Elder Brueghel (c. 1515–69), private collection), 32–33 (altarpiece by Gentile da Fabriano (c. 1370–1427), Galleria degli Uffizi, Florence, Italy), 51 (page from an illustrated children's book, 19th century, private collection), 75 (Russian icon, tempera on panel, Museum of the History of religion, St Petersburg, Russia), 80 (example of the first known Christmas card being used, 1843, hand-coloured watercolour on print by John Callcott Horsley (1817–1903), Victoria & Albert Museum, London); © National Gallery, London pp. 24, 39, 67 bottom right; Marie Claire 100 Idées 14 © Capurro p. 25 left; Maison Marie Claire 141 P62 © Primois p. 28; Hulton Getty p. 29; Aspect Picture Library/Kim Naylor p. 31; Sotheby's Picture Library London pp. 34, 45; Joseph Sammut pp. 36, 68–69, 71; Dr Janez Bogataj pp. 40, 66 (photo by J Puksic); Mary Evans Picture Library p 41; Tecwyn Vaughn-Jones p. 42 left (photo by Martin Robson Riley); National Museum of Wales pp. 42 right (photo by Frederick Evans), 44, 70 right; Ken Amer/Orkney Photographic p. 43; Garden Picture Library pp. 46 (Erika Craddock), 47 (Lynne Brotchie), 50 bottom (Friedrich Strauss), 84–85 (John Glover), 90 top & 91 (Linda Burgess); Royal Horticultural Society, Lindley Library pp. 48 (Caroline Maria Applebee), 49 (Margaret Meen); Robert Harding Syndication pp. 50 top (Jan Baldwin/Homes & Gardens),53 left (Polly Wreford/Homes & Gardens), 76–77 (Chris Drake/Country Homes & Interiors), 82–83 & 85 (Polly Wreford/Country Homes & Interiors), 86 (Marie Louise Avery/Woman & Home), 87 & 89 (Polly Wreford/Woman & Home), 90 bottom Lizzie Orme /Inspirations; Press Association/Toby Melville p. 52; Agenzia Giornalistica Italia p. 60; Austrian National Tourist Office p. 61; Panos Pictures/Sean Sprague p. 64; Elisabeth Houtzager Crib Collection pp. 65, 67 left; Ivan Lackovic Croata p. 70 left; NSPCC p. 78; Hélène Alexander, the Fan Museum p. 79; Mrs Marian Crook (photo by the late Nigel Rolstone) p. 101; BBC Worldwide p. 146; Edite Vieira p. 162. Other pictures supplied by various contributors to this book.

Thanks also to the following for providing props for photography: Goldsmith & Perris, Stand No G062, Alfie's Market, Church St, London NW8 for the loan of table silver; Habitat, Gill Wing Cookshop, 190 Upper St, London N1 and Cargo at Whiteleys of Bayswater, London W2 for china; Wedgwood of Barlaston, Stoke-on-Trent for fine china; Elaine & Sue for tablecloths; The Cutlery Shop, 5 Cavendish Place, London W1 for cutlery; Angel Flowers, 60 Upper St, London N1 for providing and arranging flowers; Urek Stolarczuk of Troika Restaurant, 101 Regents Park N1, London for preparing Polish food in his restaurant.

Finally, thanks to the following for permission to reproduce copyright material: The Oxford University Press for extracts from *The Christmas Almanac* by Michael Stephenson and from *The Oxford Christmas Book for Children* by Roderick Hunt; Dr Dunja Rihtman-Augustin of Croatia; Joseph Cassar Pullicino from *Studies in Maltese Folklore* (Malta University Press, 1992); Advantage Advertising Ltd of Malta.

Every effort has been made to trace copyright holders of material in this book. Should any omissions have been made, the publishers will be pleased to make suitable acknowledgement in future editions.